ALPHABET ACTIVITIES

Original Ideas and Worksheets for Teaching the Alphabet

Jill M. Coudron

MAKEMASTER® Blackline Masters

Fearon Teacher Aids
a division of
David S. Lake Publishers
Belmont, California

Editor: Bonnie Bernstein
Designer: Innographics
Cover designer: Joe di Chiarro
Illustrators: Sharron O'Neil and Ann Jackel
Design manager: Susan True
Production editor: Robert E. Wanetick

ISBN-0-8224-0297-1
Printed in the United States of America.
1.9 8 7

PREFACE

Alphabet Activities was written to be a companion book to *Alphabet Puppets* and *Alphabet Stories*. Together, the ideas and materials in these three books will enable you to teach letter recognition and sounds to your children through meaningful learning experiences in all curricular areas.

Alphabet Puppets introduces the idea of teaching the alphabet through puppets accompanied by stories, songs, cooking projects, and other varied learning activities. It provides patterns for making the puppets as well as ideas for incorporating the alphabet program into your classroom. It presents an effective method of teaching the alphabet that is stimulating for both the teacher and the child.

In *Alphabet Stories,* the puppets experience special adventures, which are pictorially portrayed. The letters and the sounds are carefully interwoven through the stories. Reproducible pages enable children to share the stories and puppet caricatures with their families, extending the learning beyond the classroom into the home.

Alphabet Activities presents additional learning activities, which broaden the concepts introduced in *Alphabet Puppets*. It contains many new ideas for all curricular areas, simple cooking projects in which children are actively involved, and two reproducible activity pages for each letter. A wide range of activities is available to facilitate different teaching and learning styles. Incorporated, too, are ideas that enable teachers to work with children individually, in small groups, and as a class.

CONTENTS

INTRODUCTION

Alphabet Activities is a compendium of activities designed to reinforce the learning of the alphabet for preschool, kindergarten, and primary-grade children. Activities are distributed under the following curriculum headings in each letter unit: Art, Reading and Writing Readiness, Mathematics, Science, and Movement Activities and Games. The last activity is a recipe for making an Alphabet Appetizer. In addition, there are two reproducible activity pages at the end of each unit.

The activities included in the Reading and Writing Readiness sections of this book are intended to help prepare children to be successful readers and writers. The activities encompass early learning experiences in the areas of visual discrimination, auditory discrimination, visual memory, auditory memory, fine motor control, visual and auditory sequencing, language skill development, and precomprehension skills. Specifically, these activities prepare children to read and write by teaching beginning skills such as letter, sound, and word recognition; left-to-right movement; sequencing of events; thinking and decision-making skills; and language and vocabulary development. Each activity is worked around the sound and letter of the week.

Classroom Management

Children often experiment, interact, and learn more in small groups than in full-group situations. Divide your class into small groups to work on many of the activities; it is much more feasible to have four or five children at a center watching turtles, measuring rice, playing a table game, or painting than it is to have the whole class try to do these activities at the same time. This is also helpful when supplies such as magnifying glasses, painting easels, and science materials are limited.

Teach the children responsibility while working in small groups. Have children take turns being in charge of a group, encouraging them to solve problems that arise. Often this will allow you to teach with fewer distractions.

Use this book and the ideas herein to make your

teaching a new and exciting experience. Add your own creative touches—as well as those of the children—to the activities presented.

Incorporating the Alphabet into Your Curriculum

Below is a list of general ideas and activities to help you incorporate the learning of the alphabet into your classroom curriculum.

1. Read to the children library books about subjects beginning with the letter of the week. Incorporate into the week's schedule movies and filmstrips that also feature subjects beginning with the letter.

2. Hang a large lettered sign that reads, "It is _____ week" on a wall or bulletin board. Insert the appropriate letters on the blank line each week. Before introducing the new letter on Mondays, leave the blank empty and invite the children to guess what the new letter will be.

3. Post the names of children whose first names begin with the letter of the week. Have those children help you set up the classroom activities that week.

4. Adapt simple songs, poems, and games to include your letter. For example, change the words of the song "If You're Happy and You Know It" to "If you like the letter **B**, bounce around. . . ."

5. Keep accessible a stack of flashcards for the letters you have introduced. Use them as you direct the children to line up or to go to the next activity. Present a card and ask the children to:
   - Name the letter.
   - Tell a word beginning with the letter.
   - Make the sound of the letter.
   - Find the letter in names.
   - Name the Alphabet Appetizer for the letter.

6. Keep accessible a stack of picture cards for the letters you have introduced. From time to time, present a card and ask the children to:
   - Say the sound of the beginning letter of the picture shown.
   - Name something else beginning with that sound.
   - Tell a rhyming word.

7. When the children are lining up, do the following:
   - Ask individual children to tell softly the name or sound of that week's letter.

- Pick one child to tap others to get in line quietly, saying the name of the letter of the week and having each tapped child echo it back.
- Pick one child to whisper the letter of the week to the others when they are ready.

8. Arrange field trips and classroom visitors around the alphabet program. Inform parents about upcoming letters and encourage them to visit and share their talents whenever appropriate—nurses during **Nn** week, dancers during **Dd** week, piano players during **Pp** week, and so on.

9. Teach the letter through movement and exercise. Change from one activity to another or fill small amounts of time by doing the following:
   - March around the room singing the name or sound of a letter.
   - Recite the alphabet, at the same time making an action for each letter. Do the action first and have the children repeat it.
   - Do stretching exercises, at the same time calling out the letter of the week.
   - After an activity, ask each child to sit or lie quietly. Choose someone to quietly whisper the letter of the week to the others as they prepare for the next activity.

10. Sing the name of the letter or its sound to a favorite tune. Have the children clap, jump, or use rhythm instruments to enhance this activity.

11. Prepare a "today sign" each day that tells something you are doing to help remember the letter of the week. Read the sign with the children at the beginning of each session. Choose a child to read it aloud. Ask children to find and circle the letter of the week on the sign. Put a picture of something beginning with the letter on the sign. Children will improve skills of reading left to right, recognizing high-frequency words, and sounding out words by reading a sign each day. Keep all of the signs you have used in a special box in your classroom library for children to read in their free time.

12. Use the following attention-getter to help your class become quiet and focus on you. Begin to whisper the letter of the week by yourself. As children notice what you are doing, they, too, should begin to whisper the letter with you. When everyone is whispering the letter and looking at you, tell them your message.

13. Have the children manipulate play dough to form the letter of the week and things that begin with that letter. Here is an excellent recipe that lasts well:

> 1 cup flour
> ½ cup salt
> 1 cup water
> 1 tablespoon vegetable oil
> 2 teaspoons cream of tartar
> a few drops food coloring

Mix the ingredients together and cook over low heat, stirring constantly, until the mixture forms a ball. Knead the dough for a few minutes until smooth. The play dough will keep in the refrigerator indefinitely in an airtight container. Make it pink or purple for **Pp** week, yellow for **Yy** week, and so on.

14. Encourage the children to give you ideas to help with learning the letters each week. Let them help make up new songs or verses of songs and think of activities to incorporate into your days. This demonstrates to them that you value their ideas.

ART ACTIVITIES

Aprons

Give the children six or seven paper napkins. Show them how to open them up and neatly stack them one on top of another. Use four brass fasteners to attach a ribbon about 50 inches long to the top of the napkins. If they like, the children can decorate the napkins with thin-line markers. The aprons are useful for classroom cooking. After the top napkins get dirty, the children tear them off and have clean aprons again!

Apple Trees

Have the children paint apple trees using green, red, and brown tempera paint and pieces of sponge. Have each child tell something about his or her painting. Write out what the children say in their own words, then have them find and circle the letter **A**s that appear in their recitations.

Accordion Folding

Teach the children to make accordion folds. Have each child create something that makes use of the accordion fold, such as a bird with wings or a woman wearing a skirt. Encourage the children to use their imaginations.

Apple *A*s

Provide each child with paper to draw, color, and cut out a picture of an apple. Have the children write a capital and a lower-case **A** in the middle of the apple. Put the Apple **A**s on a wall or bulletin board in the shape of a large letter **A** for a display during **Aa** week.

READING AND WRITING READINESS

Alligator Feeding

Make a large tagboard alligator with the mouth cut out. Write **A**s all over its body. Have the children take turns "feeding" it flashcards that deal with concepts you are studying, such as letter, sound, numeral, and word recognition.

Alphabet Center

Set up an alphabet center in the classroom. Include a variety of materials, such as games, alphabet books, puzzles, flashcards, and tapes or records with accompanying books.

Animal Sounds

Make the sounds of three different animals while the children listen to you. Have them repeat the three sounds in order. As they become proficient at this game, increase the number of sounds. Call the short sound of the letter **A** the "ant" sound; call the long sound of **A** the "ape" sound.

A Words

Prepare a chart or list of words on the chalkboard that have the short sound of **A**. Using your list, teach the children how to sound out words. Use simple three-letter words, such as *can, man, fat, hat, cab,* and *map*. Have the children illustrate several of these words.

MATHEMATICS ACTIVITIES

Abacus

Introduce the abacus. Let the children use it for counting by ones and tens.

Action!

On large pieces of heavy paper, print these action words: *jump, hop, skip, bend,* and *wiggle*. Print numbers on another set of cards. Have the children take turns picking a card from each pile and demonstrating the action the correct number of times.

Acorns

Collect acorns (with the children if possible) and use them at a math center for counting, learning one-to-one correspondence, forming sets, and matching objects to numbers.

SCIENCE ACTIVITIES

Aquarium

Set up an aquarium in your classroom to observe fish. Try to find an angelfish for your aquarium. Provide books and pictures of plant and animal life found in an aquarium.

Astronauts

Teach about astronauts and what they do. Have the children pretend to be astronauts and draw pictures of what they think it would be like in space. Write down their stories for them. Have them "read" the stories to you or to each other.

Air Balloons

Show the children that air takes up space by having them watch you blow up a balloon. Form a circle with the children to play a game. Have the children come into the center of the circle one at a time, say "Air begins with the letter **A**," and tap the balloon up.

MOVEMENT AND GAMES

Acrobatics

Teach the children some simple stunts, such as the log roll and forward somersault.

Angels

Have the children lay on the floor on their backs. Arms should be at their sides and legs together. At the same time, have all the children open their legs and move their arms to touch hands above heads. As a variation, have them move the arm and leg on only the left or right side of the body.

Alligators

Let the children pretend to be alligators in a swamp. Call "Alligators go!" and "Alligators stop!" When the alligators are going, they make the short sound of the letter **A**. When they are stopped, they are very quiet.

Animal Chase

Divide the class into three or four groups. Assign an animal name to each group, such as ants, alligators, apes, and angelfish. Choose one child to be the hunter. Have all the children stand in a line at one end of the play area. When the hunter calls the name of one of the animal groups, all the children that belong to that group must run to a goal line opposite where they are standing. The hunter will try to catch them by tagging them. Keep score by counting the animals caught.

Animal Actions

Cut out or draw enough pictures of animals in action so that each child can have one (some can be duplicates). Allow each child to take a turn choosing an animal picture and acting it out. Then have the entire class act out the animal's actions.

Airplane

Have the children pretend to be airplanes making the short sound of **A**. Let them zoom around the play area; do nose dives, landings, and takeoffs; and "write" **A**s in the air.

ALPHABET APPETIZER

Apple Animals

Slice apples horizontally so that each apple gives you four or five slices. Give each child one slice. Show the children how to cut out the seeds and dry the top of the slice with a paper towel. Then have them spread peanut butter or cream cheese on the slice and make an animal face using raisins, peanuts, sesame seeds, sunflower seeds, or fruit pieces. Chow mein noodles make wonderful whiskers.

APPLES ON A STRING

Color these apples. Cut them out carefully. Trace over the **A**s on them. Punch a hole where you see this mark: ⭘. String the apples on a piece of yarn. Tie the yarn and wear the apples around your neck. Let everyone hear the sound of the letter **A**!

ANTS ON THE ANTHILL

Look at each anthill. Count how many ants are crawling on each one. Write the number on the line next to the hill. Look at the top of the page if you forget how to make a number. On the back of this paper, practice writing your numbers.

 ART ACTIVITIES

Beautiful Blue Bunnies

Provide the children with bright blue tempera paint to paint bunnies. Have each child tell something special about the bunny, and write down his or her words. Let the children find the **B**s in their recitations and draw balloons around them.

Big Bugs

Give each child a small potato for the body of a bug. Provide toothpicks, pins with colored heads, pipe cleaners, buttons, and colored paper to complete the bug. Have the children give the bugs names beginning with the sound of **B**.

Blow! Blow!

Show the children how to drip paint on paper and blow through straws to move the paint around in interesting designs. When the paint is dry, have the children print a large black **B** over the colors.

Butterflies

Demonstrate how to fold a sheet of construction paper in half. Let the children drip different colors of paint on one side of the fold, then press the other side down to "print" the colors. When the paint is dry, let the children cut out a butterfly shape. Show them how to cut antennae out of the scraps and glue them on.

Boats

Give each child a sheet of construction paper. Have the children cut out the hull of a boat, a mast to hold a sail, and a sail decorated with capital and lower-case **B**s. Show them how to glue the parts together on another sheet of construction paper, then add sky and water with crayons.

 READING AND WRITING READINESS

Name Bingo

Make long cards with the children's names printed on them. As you call letters out, have the children look for them in their names. Have them use markers to cover the letters called in their names. When all the letters in a name are covered, the child calls "Bingo!" For prizes, make capital **B**s with happy faces drawn in the enclosed sections.

Book Party

Find books that deal with subjects beginning with **B**, such as bears, bunnies, bugs, and bees. Provide a special time for everyone to look at these books with friends. Make a list of the things the children found in the books that began with the letter **B**.

Books

Teach the children the importance of books during **Bb** week. Show them how to open and close a book and turn the pages, and discuss with them how books help us learn. Set aside time for everyone to enjoy books.

Beans

Give each child a handful of beans. Have the children practice forming capital and lower-case **B**s and simple picture outlines of objects beginning with **B**, such as balloons, buttons, and bunnies.

Balloons

Let the children cut out balloon shapes and attach string to them. Write a capital and lower-case **B** on each balloon for them to trace. Then ask them to write **B** words and illustrate them on the balloons.

MATHEMATICS ACTIVITIES

Buttons

Use buttons during **Bb** week for making sets; sorting by color, size, and shape; and forming numbers.

Buggy Numbers

Make patterns of the numerals 0–9. Put some kind of marking on the right side of the numeral, such as stripes or dots, so the children will not reverse the numbers. Have the children trace the patterns and make bugs by adding legs, antennae, and spots.

Back-a-Tack

Prepare a set of number cards 0–12. Pin one of the numbers on the back of a child. Have the other children in the group give clues about it, such as "It is one more than six," or "It is one less than three." Have the child wearing the number try to guess what it is.

Blocks

Have the children form numbers from blocks, and provide grid patterns to help them complete this activity. Stress beginning in the correct position and adding blocks in the same directions as when the numbers are written.

SCIENCE ACTIVITIES

Boxes

Collect a large assortment of boxes of different shapes and sizes. Ask the children to sort them, order them by size, and take off the lids and refit them. Talk about the contents of the various boxes.

Bones

Teach the children about bones. Provide books, pictures, and filmstrips explaining our skeletons and those of other animals. Have the children bring in cleaned bones from kitchen scraps or leftovers at home. Set up a bone display. Give children the opportunity to learn new things about their bones. Ask them to make a bone book in which to record what they have learned. Cut out covers and blank pages in the shape of bones for these books. Have the children share their books with each other or with another class.

Bird Feeders

Attach a string to a pine cone for each child in your class. Have the children spread peanut butter on their pine cones and roll them in birdseed. Show them how to take their bird feeders home by wrapping them in waxed paper. Hang one near the classroom so the children can observe birds around school.

MOVEMENT AND GAMES

Balance Beam

Use a balance beam to work with the children on balance and coordination. Have them practice walking frontward, backward, and sideways using slow and quick movements. Tape a **B** to the wall for the children to focus on as they work on the beam.

Body Bridges

Show the children how to make body bridges in two ways—stomachs up and backs up. Let the children work in pairs and take turns crawling under each other's bridges.

Bouncing Balls

Work with balls to develop the children's bouncing and catching skills. Ask the children to call "**B**" as they bounce.

Bicycles

Teach the children to do the bicycle exercise. Show them how to lay on their backs and hold their legs up in the air (they can use their hands to help hold themselves up). Once in position, have them move their legs as if riding a bicycle.

ALPHABET APPETIZER

Bugs on a Bed

Give each child a slice of whole wheat bread. Have the children first put "bedspreads" on their "beds" using peanut butter, cream cheese, or butter. Then have them put "bugs" on the beds using small edibles, such as raisins, nuts, cereal bits, or cut-up fruits or vegetables. Use this project for counting practice by having the children count the number of bugs they put on the bread. Pita, or pocket, bread will work well for this cooking project, too, in which case call it "Bugs *in* a Bed."

BALLOON BOOK

Cut out each of the pages below. Read what color it says to color the balloon. Color each balloon. Put your book together. Trace the letters on your cover and decorate it. Write your name on the cover. Read your book to someone.

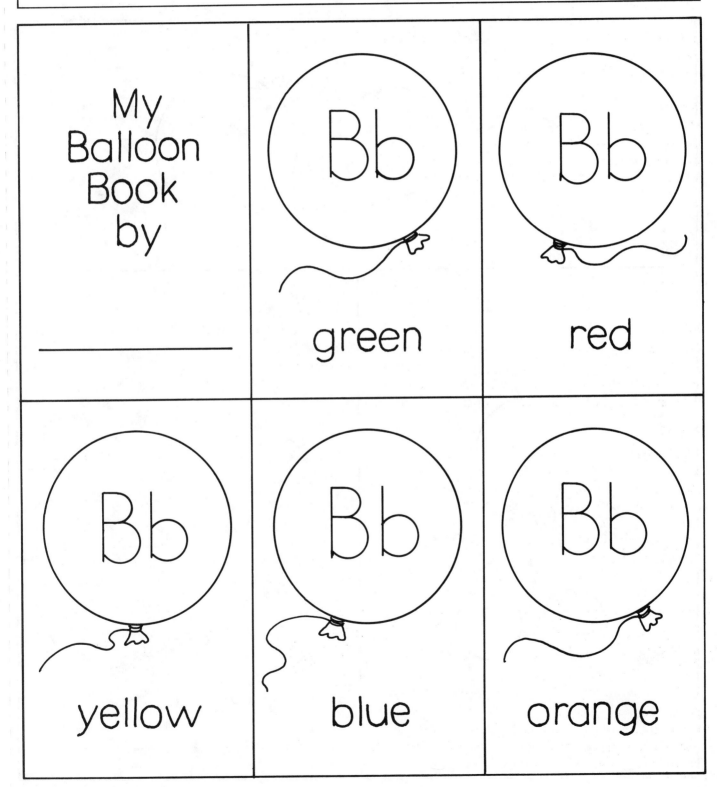

My
Balloon
Book
by

_____

green

red

yellow

blue

orange

BROWN BEAR

Cut out the circle patterns. Make a bear like the one on this page. Trace two small circles for ears, four medium-size circles for arms and legs, and two large circles for the head and body. Then color your bear brown and give it a face, a bow tie, buttons, and **B**s. On the back of this page, use the circle patterns to make other animals.

Cc

Clothespin Creations

Show the children how to make clothespin people by decorating clothespins with paper, glue, markers, yarn, and other items you have on hand. Have the children put on a show with the creatures they make.

Colorful Clowns

Have the children draw and color or paint large, happy clown faces, then cut them out. Give each child a halved styrofoam ball to paint bright red and to glue onto the clown face for a three-dimensional nose.

Curly Caterpillars

Show the children how to glue 1½-by-8-inch colored construction-paper strips into rings, then glue six or seven rings together to form a long caterpillar. Suggest that they add faces, antennae, and other features.

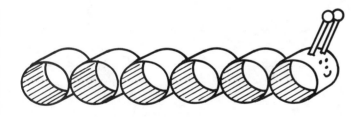

Colorful Collage

Have the children cut out pictures of colorful things. Let them glue their pictures to a large paper **C** to make a classroom collage as a display for **Cc** week.

Calico Cats

Provide fabric or wallpaper for cutting out the head and body of a cat. Have the children add features with markers and crayons. Ask the children to tell you stories about their cats. Write down the stories in their own words; then have the children find and circle all the **C**s in their recitations.

Comics

Cut out the frames of suitable comic strips and put them into envelopes. Have the children use them for practice in sequencing and storytelling. Back the frames with heavy paper, then laminate them or cover them with clear contact paper.

C Hunt

Ask the children to look for all the things they can find in the classroom that begin with the letter **C**. List them on a chart.

Clap for C

Have the children sit in a group around you as you say words. Have them clap if you say a word beginning with the hard sound of **C**. If you say a word that does not have the hard sound of **C**, have them shake their heads.

Cutouts

Ask the children to cut out pictures from newspapers and magazines of things that begin with the letter **C**. Have them glue the pictures onto sheets of paper and print a capital and a lower-case **C** on the page.

Coupons

Provide the children with little sheets of paper. Help them write or draw pictures of favors they can do at home. For example, they might make coupons for a hug, a kiss, a table set, a room cleaned, vacuuming, or taking care of a younger brother or sister. Let them decorate envelopes to take the coupons home in.

Counting

Provide **C** things, such as cotton balls, clips, cups, and clothespins, for the children to use to practice their counting skills. Make a set of paper plates numbered 0–12 for the children to count out the objects on.

Cards

Place decks of playing cards at a work area. Let the children use the cards for matching numbers, ordering, and sorting by suits and numbers. Teach the children some simple games, such as "Go Fish" and "War."

Clocks

Work with children in small groups, teaching them about the clock and how to tell time on the hour and the half-hour. Show each child how to make a clock using a paper plate, two paper hands, and a brass fastener.

Clothesline Game

Hang up a string or rope in your classroom. With clothespins, arrange some articles of clothing on the line. Blindfold one child and change the arrangement of the articles. The blindfolded child must put the things back in the correct order. After using clothing, pin large cut-out numbers to the line in different arrangements for reordering.

SCIENCE ACTIVITIES

Classifying Clothing

Cut out pictures of different kinds of clothing. Ask the children to sort the pictures according to warm and cold weather, work and play, or body parts.

Carrot Tops

Provide a carrot and a small container for each child. Demonstrate how to cut the carrot so that just an inch of the top remains. Lay the top in a dish of water and observe what happens. Have the children keep water in their dishes.

Caterpillars and Cocoons

Teach the children facts about caterpillars and cocoons. Bring some in for observation with magnifying glasses. Provide books, pictures, and filmstrips on the subject to extend the children's learning.

MOVEMENT AND GAMES

Clip Relay

Divide the class into teams. Give each child a clip clothespin to hold. To play, the children pass a card with a **C** printed on it down the lines of their teams by clipping and unclipping the card until it reaches the last child. The first team to finish should sit down and quietly make the sound of **C**. Ask the children to say "**C**" as they pass the card to each other.

Cave

Make a cave in one corner of the play area by draping sheets or blankets over some tables. Let the children pretend to be caterpillars crawling in and out of the cave. Ask them to make the hard sound of **C** as they crawl around.

Catching

Cut off the tops of plastic milk jugs with handles to use as receptacles for catching balls and beanbags that the children throw. Help the children use their eyes and hands while throwing and catching.

Climbing

Take the children to a play area where there is climbing equipment such as bars and jungle gyms. Ask them to call out "**C**!" when they reach the top of a climbing structure.

ALPHABET APPETIZER

Crazy Caterpillar Critters

For this snack project, provide a variety of vegetables that begin with the letter **C**, such as celery, carrots, cucumbers, cabbage, and cauliflower. Let the children help cut these into small pieces and rounds. Have them assemble a caterpillar in the shape of a **C** by sticking the vegetables together with peanut butter or cream cheese. Give each child a large piece of cabbage to be the "grass" under the crazy critter.

CATERPILLAR CAPERS

Find all the circles with the letter **C** on them. Cut them out. Glue them onto another sheet of paper to make a long caterpillar. Color your caterpillar and make a home for it by drawing grass, trees, flowers, and a rock for it to crawl on. Trace over the **C**s on the circles with a crayon.

COUNT
AND
COLOR

Count and color the pictures in each box. Circle all the **C**s you see on the page and trace the **C**s in the last box. On the back of this paper, draw and color five things that begin with **C**.

Color 1 cup red.

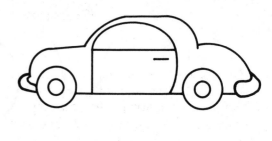
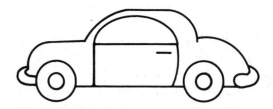

Color 2 cars blue.

Color 3 cakes yellow.

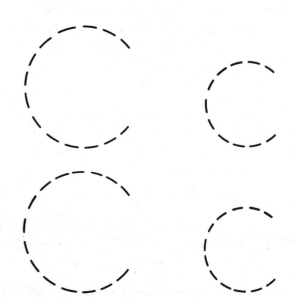

Trace 4 letter C's.

ART
ACTIVITIES

Daisies

Have the children cut out a circle and glue it to the center of a sheet of construction paper. Show them how to cut petals in a variety of colors and glue them around the circle to form a daisy. Have the children add stems, leaves, and other decorations.

Decorated Dragon

Give each child a paper plate to decorate for a scale on a long dragon. Assemble the dragon on a classroom wall or bulletin board. Make a dragon face with fire coming out of the nostrils. With the children, choose a name for the dragon beginning with the letter **D**. Have the children tell the class stories about the dragon.

Donut *D*

Give each child a sheet of paper. Have the children cut out donut shapes and decorate them. Form these donuts into the shape of a large capital **D** for your wall or bulletin board as a display for **Dd** week.

Dads

Ask the children to draw and color large pictures of their dads (or another significant male figure if there is no dad). Have them tell you something special about their dads to write down on the pictures.

Decorated Door

Ask each child to design and cut out a special **D**. Decorate the door of your classroom with the **D**s.

Dotty *D*s

Prepare a capital and a lower-case **D** for each child to cut out. Have the children make dots all over the **D**s. Put them in a display for **Dd** week.

Dip and Dye

Demonstrate to the children how to fold pieces of paper towels three or four times. Pour food coloring diluted with water into small containers. Show the children how to dip the corners of their folded towels into the different colors, turning the towel to color each corner. Press the toweling between newspaper to squeeze out the excess moisture. Open the towel and let it dry on newspaper.

Doodlies

Have the children scribble on sheets of paper with black crayons. Have them look for face shapes in the doodles and draw in little eyes, noses, and mouths. Call them "Doodlies."

READING AND
WRITING READINESS

Word Dice

Provide large blocks to use as dice. On the sides of the dice, print high-frequency words that you want the children to learn. Teach the children how to tally by shaking the dice and watching for a particular word. For example, if the word *the* is designated, each time they roll *the*, they tally a point. This game can be adapted to color words, numbers, or letters.

Dictionary

Teach the children to use a simple dictionary. Have them look in the **D** section, writing down and illustrating words that begin with **D**.

D Words

Provide plastic cups or margarine tubs as containers. In each container, cut up the letters of a **D** word. Print the word on the outside of the container so that the children can match the letters inside to the word on the outside to make a word and read it.

d or *b*?

Teach the children the difference between lower-case **b** and **d**. Show them that lower-case **b** is "hiding" in capital **B**. Explain to them that they can watch for the stick and the ball: For a **b**, the stick comes before the ball; for a **d**, the stick comes after the ball.

MATHEMATICS ACTIVITIES

Dice

Using wooden blocks, make a pair of dice for the children to use with counting, set recognition, and adding. On one of the dice, write the numerals you are studying; on the other, make the sets. Have the children take turns throwing the dice to try and match a numeral with a set.

Dimes

Bring in dimes for the children to inspect and handle. Have them use the dimes to practice counting by tens. Provide other coins for the children to compare with the dimes.

Dozen

Teach the children how many are in a dozen. Give each child an empty egg carton to count the sections. Have the children write the numeral 12. Give them markers or beans to count out into the sections of the egg carton.

Diamond

Teach the children to make the diamond shape. Show them how to measure and make a mark halfway across each side of an 8½-by-11-inch sheet of paper. Have them connect the marks to form the diamond shape. Have them draw something that begins with the letter **D** inside the diamond.

SCIENCE ACTIVITIES

Dinosaurs

Provide books, filmstrips, and pictures of different kinds of dinosaurs. Mark off a space on the playground or in the gym to show how long a dinosaur was. Have the children draw or paint dinosaurs or mold them out of clay.

Dirt

Give each child a cup and some dirt in which to plant a flower or vegetable seed. Ask them to keep it in a sunny spot and keep it watered. Have the children watch the progress of the plants' growth.

Dogs

Teach the children about different kinds of dogs. Provide books with pictures of all kinds of dogs. Encourage children who have dogs to let them visit the classroom. Keep a chart of all the visitors and a sentence about each of them.

MOVEMENT AND GAMES

Dragon Hunt

Ask the children to pretend that they must find a terrible dizzy dotted dragon, who is living in a cave. Choose someone to be the dragon. While the rest of the class closes their eyes, the dragon hides somewhere in the play area. Give the signal "Find the Dragon!" to send the children searching for the dragon. When they find the dragon, they run back to a designated safe area. The dragon tries to tag someone who will become the dragon for the next game.

Dodge Ball

Have the children form a circle facing inward. Choose three children to go inside the circle. The other children throw balls into the center, trying to touch one of the inside children. If they are successful, they exchange places with the children they hit.

Ducks

Have the children pretend to be ducks out for a walk on a nice day. As they waddle about, ask them to make the sound of **D**.

ALPHABET APPETIZER

Dirt Dessert

Give each child a small paper cup with ½ cup vanilla yogurt. Let them measure and crush ¼ cup granola and sprinkle it over the yogurt for "dirt." Have the children make paper flowers attached to straws to stick into the dessert before serving. Refrigerate or freeze before serving. For variation, substitute pudding or ice cream for the vanilla yogurt.

BE A DETECTIVE

Look at the picture inside each spyglass. If the picture begins with the letter **D**, print a capital and a lower-case **D** on the line beside it. If it does not begin with a **D**, write "not **D**." On the back of this paper, practice writing your capital and lower-case **D**s.

DOGGIE GROW

Cut out the front and back of the dog. Cut out the number squares. Make a game by laying out the dog's front, then the numbers in order, and then the end of the dog. Keep the parts in an envelope, or glue them down onto a sheet of paper.

ART ACTIVITIES

Embroidery

Cut old sheets or other material into 5-by-7-inch rectangles. Teach the children to sew on the lines of pictures you draw on the material. Make capital and lower-case **E**s, elephants, and decorated eggs for the children to choose from.

Hatching Eggs

Have each child cut out an oval shape for an egg. Show the children how to cut jaggedly across the middle of the egg to make it look cracked. Have them make a baby chick to fit inside the egg. With a brass fastener, connect the bird with both halves of the egg at the bottom. The egg "opens" to hatch.

Eggs

Collect plastic eggs (hosiery containers or prize containers in some gum ball machines). Let the children glue Easter-egg grass in half of an egg. Show them how to make a chick by gluing two cotton balls together and making a tiny face on the top ball. Have them put their chicks in their eggs and use markers to decorate the outsides of the eggs.

Eskimos

Ask the children to cut out large round shapes for the faces of Eskimos. Show them how to glue white cut-out circles around the face for the fur of a hood. Have them glue or color on other features. Talk about why Eskimos need to be dressed in warm clothing.

READING AND WRITING READINESS

Envelopes

Prepare some envelopes with **E** words printed on them, such as *exit, end, elephant, egg, elf, elevator, echo, exercise,* and *empty*. Draw or cut out small pictures representing each word, and paste the pictures on the outside of the envelope, too. Make 1-inch-square cards, each displaying a letter from a word on one of the envelopes. Put the letters into the appropriate envelopes. Let the children arrange the letter cards to form the words on the envelopes.

Erase-a-Word

Divide the chalkboard in half for this relay game. Print lists of the same words on each side of the board. Use words you are teaching, such as high-frequency words, color words, or number words. When you give the signal "**E**!" one child from each team goes to the board, reads a word, erases it, runs back, and tags the next child in line, calling "**E**!" The first team with all the words erased is the winner.

Let's Eat!

Have the children listen carefully as you read a list of words. If the word is something to eat, have the children clap their hands and say "**E**!"

Echo Game

Have the children listen to and repeat sentences that you say exactly as you say them. Use sentences with many **E** words in them. *Examples:* "An elephant went skating and fell down eleven times"; "Ed painted a picture of an elk and an eagle."

MATHEMATICS ACTIVITIES

Help the Elf

Make an elf with a bag that the children can easily reach into, and pin it onto your bulletin board. Attach number cards to the bulletin board by paper-punching holes in the cards and hanging them on pins. As the children name the numbers, they take them off the board and put them into the elf's bag. Have them play the game in reverse and name the numbers as they put them back onto the pins.

Egg Cartons

Provide egg cartons for counting and making sets. Write numbers in the bottoms of the cups. Have the children count the correct number of beans, buttons, or markers into the sections.

Equal

Teach the children the mathematical term *equal*. Show them what an equals sign looks like. Talk about its relationship to the terms *greater than* and *less than* and what it means in simple arithmetic. Ask the children to solve simple problems using the equals sign.

SCIENCE ACTIVITIES

Eggs

With the children, observe some eggs hatching in a classroom incubator. After the chicks have hatched and the children have had time to observe them, give them to a farm. Have the children compile a book relating the steps of the eggs' being hatched.

Electricity

Cut out pictures of things that do and do not use electricity. Ask the children to sort the pictures. Discuss with the children how the electrical devices are used. Let the children look in magazines for pictures of electrical devices, and have them cut them out.

Expert

Invite an electrician into your classroom to talk to the children about his or her work. Ask the electrician to conduct some experiments for the children to watch.

MOVEMENT AND GAMES

E Movements

Let the children move about the play area as eagles, elephants, and eels. Encourage them to be creative.

Egg Rolls

Teach the children how to do "egg rolls" on mats. Have them begin in a sitting position with their knees up. Have them roll sideways down the mats holding their knees tightly with their arms.

Exercises

Do exercises with the children. Try jumping jacks, deep knee bends, sit-ups, and toe touchers. Call out "**E**!" as you exercise.

Exercise Shapes

Have the children make shapes with their bodies. For circles, have them roll their bodies into balls. Let them stretch out to make lines. Have them sit on the floor and touch their toes to make triangles. To make rectangles, have a pair of children lie on their sides and stretch out their arms in front of them while holding on to each other's ankles. Try to have everyone in the class help make a giant square, circle, triangle, and rectangle.

Elves

Have the children try and make themselves small and walk around as little elves. Have them greet each other with the short sound of **E**.

ALPHABET APPETIZER

Egg Boats

Hard-boil one egg for every two children in the class. Have the children work in pairs to peel the shell from the egg, slice the egg in half, then carefully remove the yolk and put it in a small paper cup. Have each pair mix the yolk with 1 teaspoon mayonnaise, ½ teaspoon mustard, and a dash of salt and pepper. This mixture is scooped back into the hollows of the white. Have each child make a sail for the boat with a toothpick and a paper flag with a capital and lowercase **E** on it; have them stick the sails into their egg boats.

EGGS IN A BASKET

Color and decorate the basket. Cut it out and fold it away from you on the dotted line. Staple the sides together. Trace the **E**s on the eggs. Cut out the eggs and put them in your basket.

EGG PUZZLES

Make your own egg puzzles. Cut out the eggs carefully. Then cut each egg apart on the dotted line. Put the pieces of the eggs into an envelope. Take them out and solve the egg puzzles.

Ff

Finger Painting

Have the children finger-paint **F**s and things that begin with **F**, such as fish, flowers, frogs, and feathers.

Fancy Fish with Freckles

Ask the children to paint brightly colored fish in blue water. Have them freckle their fish with different colors of paint. Have the children tell you something special about their fish. Write it down in their own words, then have them find and circle all the **F**s in their recitations.

Frames

Show the children how to make a frame for a picture by cutting out the middle of a sheet of colored construction paper. Glue this over a sheet of drawing paper of the same size. Have the children draw a picture of the letter **F** or something beginning with the letter **F** inside the frame.

Fantastic Flower

Cut out a petal for each child to decorate. Arrange the petals into a giant class flower by affixing each child's petal around a paper circle with a capital and a lower-case **F** printed on it. Pin the fantastic flower to a wall or a bulletin board.

Making Faces

Divide the class into small groups. Give each group a large sheet of paper. Have the children in each group take turns drawing in a feature of a face. When the groups have made complete faces, let them share the pictures with each other. Display the faces during **Ff** week with the caption "**F** Is for Faces."

Funny Painting

Let the children experiment with painting with forks, feathers, fingers, and feet instead of paintbrushes.

Feet

Have each child trace and cut out the shape of one of his or her feet. Form a large capital and a lower-case **F** from the cut-out feet for an **Ff**-week display.

Flower Arranging

Ask parents to send unwanted artificial flowers to school, with which the children can make decorative floral arrangements. Provide plastic jars and oatmeal boxes as vases. If the children enjoy this activity, ask other school personnel to send "orders" to fill. Encourage them to print color words and numerals on the orders to help the children extend their learning.

Folding

Provide square and rectangular pieces of material, washcloths, towels, and scrap paper for this activity. Teach the children to fold by matching corners. Let them practice using the materials provided.

Friend Books

Have the children design books of their friends. Ask them to draw a picture and write the name of a different friend on each page. Have them design covers and print the words "My Friend Book by
_____ ." To help the children with this activity, make a flashcard with each child's name and a small photograph. Display the names on a pocket chart.

Feeling

Using a large box with a lid, prepare a "Feeling Box" for the classroom. Cut a hole in the center of the lid, and sew or staple in a long sock with the toe cut out. Cover the box with bright contact paper. Fill the box with items that are small enough to slip through the sock. Working in small groups, have the children take turns putting their hands through the sock and getting an object. Ask them to identify it using only their sense of touch. After they guess, ask them to take the object out to see if they were correct.

Funny *F*s

Give the children big sheets of paper to make funny **F**s. Print a capital and a lower-case **F** on each paper so the children have the pattern to look at as they make **F**s with curvy, crooked, and silly lines.

MATHEMATICS ACTIVITIES

F Numerals

Study the numerals 4, 5, 14, and 15 with the children. Have the children practice making sets of these numbers counting feathers, forks, flowers, and cut-out feet. Ask them to practice writing the numerals and constructing them from blocks, beads, or bottle caps. Let the children draw sets of flowers and fish to represent these numbers.

Flour

Provide flour in cake pans for the children to practice writing numerals and forming geometric shapes.

Find the Face

Cut out a large numeral for each two children in the class. Make a large face on the numeral and cut it apart. Mix up the numeral parts and distribute one part to each child. Explain that when you make the sound of **F**, they are to find the child with the other half of their numeral, completing the face at the same time. After the game, put the numeral pieces in a box for the children to use as puzzles in their free time.

SCIENCE ACTIVITIES

Floating

Provide different articles—for example, corks, paper clips, bottle caps, or plastic clasps—for the children to test in water to see if they float. Have the class make a chart by drawing pictures of the things that floated.

Fruits

Ask each of the children to bring a fresh fruit to school. Examine the fruits, classify them according to color and size, notice their likenesses and differences, and discuss the inside and outside of each. Have the children help cut them up into bite-size pieces to have a "fruit feast."

Funnels

Collect funnels of different sizes. Set up a sand or water center for the children to explore the use of funnels. Provide various containers for pouring.

Food

Teach the children about the food groups. Let them look at pictures and discuss the importance of eating food from each group each day. Make a class chart for the food groups. Have the children look in magazines and cut out food pictures for each group on the chart. Provide a food sample from each group.

MOVEMENT AND GAMES

Feet

Have the children explore all the movements of feet, such as walking, dancing, galloping, hopping, skipping, jumping, kicking, and tiptoeing. If the environment is safe, let the children explore with bare feet.

Freeze

Call out movements for the children to perform, such as walk, run, skip, hop, duckwalk, whirl, and jump. When you call "Freeze!" they must stop immediately and hold the positions they are in.

Fire Engine

Count off the children by fours. Explain that they are now fire stations number one, two, three, and four. Choose someone to be the chief. When the chief calls out a fire station number, the children from that group run to a designated area and pretend to put out a fire, holding imaginary hoses and making the sound of **F**. When the chief calls, "All Fire Stations!" all the children run to put out the fire.

ALPHABET APPETIZER

Funny Faces with Fruit

Provide for each child a halved orange in the shell. Have each child carefully scoop out the insides of the orange, draw a funny face on the outside of the orange shell with a marker, and then cut up the scooped-out orange into bite-size pieces and put them back into the shell. Have the children help you cut up other fruits, such as apples, bananas, and pears. Let the children mix these fruits with the orange pieces. Use a toothpick to eat the fruit.

FISH FOR
F AND f

Look at the fish in the sea. Some of them have the letter **F** or **f** on them. Draw a circle around the fishes with **F**s and trace over the **F**s. On the back of this paper, draw some fancy fish of your own with **F** and **f** on them. Have fun!

FUNNY FLOWERS

Look at the funny flowers. Some of the pictures do not go with the letters on the leaves. Cross out those flowers. Then color the flowers whose pictures begin with the sound on the leaves. On the back of this paper, draw five flowers. Write **F**s on them.

Alphabet Activities reproducible page, copyright © 1983

ART ACTIVITIES

Green Green Green

Mix various shades of green tempera paint for the art center. Have the children paint designs and pictures. Write down interesting things they tell you about their pictures. Ask them to find all the **G**s in their recitations and make a little ghost around each of them.

Goofy Guys and Gals

Collect empty thread spools so that each child has two or three to work with. Show them how to glue the spools together one on top of another. Have the children draw eyes, noses, and mouths with markers and attach paper arms, legs, and hair with glue. Use other materials to decorate, such as yarn, sewing trims, and buttons.

Globs of Glue

Show the children how to spill a glob of glue onto a sheet of waxed paper. Let this dry until it is hard and clear Using thin-line markers, have the children decorate their globs. Have them peel the globs off the waxed paper and hang them from the light fixtures or in windows.

Groovy Gloves

Have the children trace around the fingers of both their hands to make a pair of gloves. Let them decorate the gloves with capital and lower-case **G**s and other designs. Make a large **G**, formed from the gloves they have cut out, for the bulletin board or wall.

Goodies Under Glass

Provide a small jar (such as a baby food jar) for each child. Have the children stick small mounds of clay in the lids. Ask them to create small pictures or **G** designs on heavy paper to stand up in the clay. Have them close the jars over the lids and print **G**s on the glass with a permanent marker.

Ghosts

On dark paper, have the children paint white ghosts. When the ghosts are dry, ask the children to tell goofy stories about their ghosts to the class.

READING AND WRITING READINESS

Go Get

Give a single direction or a series of directions telling children to get things for you. Remind the children to listen very carefully because sometimes you will ask them to bring you things that will be impossible, such as the ceiling, an elephant, or the chalkboard. Ask them to bring chalk, erasers, books, games, blocks, toys, and a coat.

Ghostly *ABC*s

Tell the children to recite the alphabet as if they were ghosts, using spooky, eerie voices. Ask them to clap on the letter **G**. Tell the ghostly voices to count, too.

Growing Green

Have the children pretend they are something green that will grow. As you read a list of words, ask them to ''grow'' whenever they hear a word beginning with the hard sound of **G**.

*G*s on a Ghost

Teach the children how to make a capital and a lower-case **G**. Have them practice on scratch paper or the chalkboard. Give them each a sheet you have prepared with a large and a small ghost. Have them print capital **G**s on the large ghost and lower-case **G**s on the small ghost.

A garden of *G*s

Give the children sheets of paper. Ask them to draw lines on the bottom as stems of flowers. Instead of flowers, ask them to make capital and lower-case **G**s on the stems.

MATHEMATICS ACTIVITIES

Graphing

Show a graph to the children and explain what it is. Make some class graphs showing favorite colors, eye colors, and hair colors; the numbers of boys and girls; and how many children have a **G** in their name. Have the children make graphs of their own.

Grocery Store

Set up a pretend grocery store in the classroom. Let the children help by bringing in empty cans and boxes. Put a play cash register in the store. Have the children make signs and price tags using crayons, markers, paper, and tape. Ask the children to bring toy grocery carts from home. Use toy or real money in the cash register.

Ghost Game

Play this game with small groups of children. Make a large ghost and cut it apart like a puzzle. Write a number on each section. Begin with the ghost put together. Let the children take turns making the ghost "disappear" by taking out a section and naming the number on it. Play the game in reverse by putting the ghost back together.

SCIENCE ACTIVITIES

Growing Grass

Provide half an eggshell for each child to draw a silly face on with a marker. Let them spoon a little soil into the shell, sprinkle grass seed over the soil, and cover the seeds with a little more soil. Let them water the grass as needed with a spoon or eyedropper. Tell the children to give their grass a "haircut" if it gets long enough. Have the children take the grass home and plant it in their own yards.

Grapes

Provide several grapes for each child, along with a small piece of aluminum foil with his or her name on it. Have the children place the grapes on the foil and observe what happens to the grapes over a period of

two weeks. Have the children make little books to record the changes in the grapes. Help them write the words in the books.

MOVEMENT AND GAMES

Movements for G

Have the children do interpretive movement on the play area as gorillas, ghosts, waddling geese, golfers, grasshoppers, and rolling grapes.

Galloping

Teach the children to gallop by running while keeping one foot extended in front of them. Have them gallop to music and in races around the play area.

Get-Ups

Show the children how to sit back-to-back in twos, on a mat, with their arms linked together. Ask them to try to get up while holding onto each other. If they are successful, have them call out "G!"

Goldfish

Have the children pretend to be goldfish. Tell them to imagine the gym or play area is their bowl. Ask them to swim quietly around, stop occasionally to rest, swim high and low, and stop and look at each other. Have the goldfish quietly greet each other by making the hard sound of **G**.

ALPHABET APPETIZER

Guy or Gal Salad

Have each child wash and dry a piece of lettuce and set it on a plate. Give each a peach half to cut in half again. The halves should be arranged on the lettuce, one above the other but touching, to form a head and body. Next, have the children insert two thin celery or carrot sticks for arms and two for legs into the bottom peach section. Tell them to make a face with raisins in the top peach section and to put hair around the top, using shredded cheddar cheese or cottage cheese for the hair.

GHOSTS, GHOSTS!

Look at the pairs of ghosts. In each pair the number on one ghost is greater than the number on the other ghost. Circle the ghost with the greater number. On the back of this paper, make three pairs of your own ghosts. Put numbers on them and circle the ghosts with the greater numbers.

LET'S GO!

Cut out the pages below. Color in the illustrations. Write your name on the title page. Write **G**s on the backs of the pages. Put your book together and practice reading.

Let's Go! By _____

Let's go to a  .

Let's go to a  .

Let's go to a  .

Let's go to the 〜〜〜 .

Let's go to 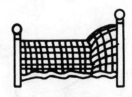 .

 **ART ACTIVITIES**

Humpty Dumpty

Have the children draw and cut out a large oval shape for an egg. Have them color on faces and cut out paper arms and legs to glue onto the egg. Have them glue Humpty Dumpty onto a sheet of paper on which they have written capital and lowercase **H**s.

Hands

Ask the children to carefully trace one of their hands and cut out the tracing. Have them write their names on the cutouts and keep them to attach to and identify artwork throughout the year.

Hearts

Teach the children how to cut out hearts. Do this in one of these ways: (1) Draw candy canes and cut. (2) Draw humps on a **V** and cut. (3) Trace around the thumb on a fold and cut. Have the children cut out hearts of many different shapes, sizes, and colors. Let them glue them together to form interesting creatures or designs.

Miniature Hats

Prepare hats for the class to decorate by melting styrofoam cups in a 350° oven. Place the cups on a cookie sheet and set them in the oven for 30–60 seconds. Watch them carefully, because they shrink quickly. Have the children decorate them by drawing on them with markers and by tying yarn or ribbon around them. Hang them from a tree branch for a display during **Hh** week.

Hammer Art

Give each child an aluminum pie plate. Have the children draw pictures on their plates with pencils. Then have them use a hammer and nail to puncture the pie plate along the pencil markings. Hang the hammer art from the light fixtures or in the windows of the classroom. Encourage the children to hammer an **H** somewhere in the picture.

Hand-Print Birds

Have the children color birds in bright colors on large sheets of paper. Let them dip one hand in paint and "print" a wing on each side of the bird's body.

 **READING AND WRITING READINESS**

Hear and Hunt

Divide the children into two teams and give each team a name beginning with the letter **H**. Blindfold one child from each team. Choose someone else to ring a bell. Ask both blindfolded children to try to locate the person with the bell. The child who is first to do so scores a point for the team.

Horns

Play this game in the same manner as "Simon Says." Have the children sit in a circle with their hands on a table or on their knees. Say, "All horns up," or "Cat's horns up," or "Bull's horns up," and so forth. If the children put their "horns" (that is, their hands) up for an animal that does not have horns, they are out of the game. Some animals with horns are rhinoceros, elk, bull, moose, goat, antelope, deer, and buffalo.

Sound of *H*

Teach the sound of the letter **H** as the sound a puppy makes when it has been running hard. Ask the children to put their hands in front of their mouths to feel the air as they make the sound of **H**. Give each child two small cards. Ask them to write "**H**" on one and "not **H**" on the other. Read the following list of words to them. Tell them to hold up the correct card—"**H**" or "not **H**"—as you say each word.

hot	will	night	tight	open
not	happy	mist	hold	he
fall	heavy	violet	heart	wheel
got	hard	hole	make	ham

MATHEMATICS ACTIVITIES

Hundred

Talk with the children about how many 100 is. Write the numeral on the board. With the children, count to 100. Provide counters for the children to count to 100. Have them write the numeral.

Humpty Dumpty

While working with a small group of children, choose one to be Humpty. Have Humpty sit on a chair that represents the wall. Show flashcards to Humpty with numbers, geometric shapes, or addition or subtraction problems. Have Humpty sit on the wall until he or she makes a mistake. Give each child a turn to be Humpty.

How High?

Give the children opportunities to show you how high they are able to count aloud. Have them write the numbers as far as they can go.

Hands and Numbers

Ask the children to trace both their hands onto a large sheet of paper. Tell them to number the tracings of their fingers, beginning at the left. Have them draw on fingernails, rings, and lines.

SCIENCE ACTIVITIES

Hibernation

Teach the children about animals that hibernate. Collect books and pictures about hibernation for the children to look at. Show the children the following experiment and then let them try it: Cut out a piece of newspaper in the shape of a small bear. Fold in the arms, legs, and head as a bear would tuck them in to sleep. Put the folded bear gently in a tub of water. The bear will unfold, or "wake up," just as real bears do when they come out of hibernation.

Heat

Discuss with the children how different foods are changed by heat. Let the children help as much as possible in cooking one or more foods to observe the changes. Good foods to observe are hamburgers, apples, bread, eggs, popcorn, or rice. Talk about the changes as they are happening in the cooking process—size, color, shape, and smell. Let the children make a "Before and After" picture of each food prepared.

MOVEMENT AND GAMES

Hop the *H*

Tape or chalk a large **H** on the floor. Have the children stand in a circle. Choose one child to begin the game by going to the center of the circle to hop on the lines of the **H**. Ask the children to make the sound of **H** as they hop. the first child taps the next person to take his or her place, saying "**H**" at the same time.

Hopping Trail

Press down contact-paper foot shapes along a play area or in the gym. Let the children hop along the trail, making the sound of **H** as they go.

High-Stepping Horses

Put some prancing music on the record or tape player, and have the children move like horses, bringing their knees up high on each step. When the music stops, have the horses stop. Tell them to greet each other with an "**H**!" while prancing.

Horseshoes

Have the children throw plastic horseshoes or screw bands from canning jars around a stick embedded in clay.

ALPHABET APPETIZER

Happy Hamburgers

Provide each child with a small bun half or biscuit and a ball of hamburger (about ¼ cup). Have the children form a patty from the ball of hamburger and fry the patty on both sides (with your help) until it is done. Have them place the cooked hamburgers on the buns and give the hamburgers happy faces by decorating them with cheese chunks, carrot and celery pieces, or ketchup and mustard.

HATS FOR HEADS

Cut out the hats at the bottom of the page. Look at the picture on each one. Match it to the head with the same letter the picture begins with. Color and decorate the hats and faces when you are finished. On the back of this paper, design a hat to wear to a haunted house.

MAKE A HOUSE

Cut out the squares on the bottom of the page. Glue them onto the house, matching them with the dotted-line squares. Trace around the house when you are finished. Trace the capital and lower-case **H**s on the house. On the back of this paper, make a capital and a lower-case **H** of your own.

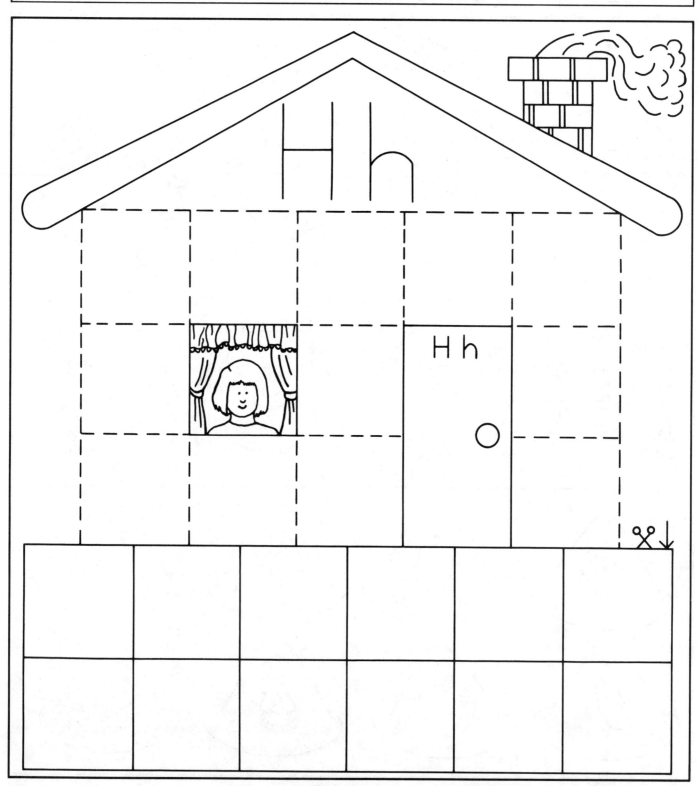

ART ACTIVITIES

Inchworms

Show the children how to make inchworms by cutting an egg carton in half the long way. Let children add spots, stripes, and other features with paint or markers. Give each child two pipe cleaners to stick into the front for antennae.

Ink Designs

Demonstrate to the children how to dip sticks into ink to make pictures or designs. Ask them to make a capital and a lower-case **I** somewhere on their pictures.

Imaginary Playground

First, ask the children to imagine what a finger playground would be. You may wish to brainstorm as a class. Then have them use paper in a variety of ways to make playground toys for fingers, such as curling paper, cutting spirals, loops, rings, strips glued in different formations, or any other creative uses they can think of. Give children the opportunity to show and tell about the playgrounds they have made.

Idea Pictures

Give each child the same small object, such as a button, paper clip, sewing trim, sequin, coin, or cork, to glue onto a sheet of construction paper. Have the children create pictures around the object. Encourage them to show their pictures to each other.

Ironed Pictures

Show the children how to fold a paper in half and color heavily on half of the paper, making a picture or a design. Help them fold the paper together and press with a hot iron. The picture will transfer to the other half of the paper.

Ironed *I*s

Have the children color capital and lower-case **I**s onto pieces of material or old sheeting. Show them how to set colors by placing the material between sheets of newspaper and pressing with a hot iron.

Igloos

Have the children paint or draw white igloos on dark paper. Ask them to draw someone beside the igloo. Have the children tell little stories about their igloos. Write down each child's story on his or her paper, and have them find **I**s in the text of their recitations and make ice-cube squares around them.

READING AND WRITING READINESS

Indian Drum

Recite nursery rhymes for the class, beating out the rhythm on a drum. Then beat the rhythm of some rhyme without saying the words and have the children identify the rhyme.

Indian Feather Game

Play this game with small groups of children. Make a 9-by-12-inch card for each child, using a different color for each. On each card, draw an Indian boy or girl wearing a headband and a set of six feathers. Print a color word you are teaching on each feather. Make each card's words a little different. Cut out paper or felt feathers to match all the color words on the feathers. Place these within reach of all the children playing the game. Prepare a spinner with the color words on sections around it. Teach the children to take turns by spinning the spinner, reading the word, and looking on their sets of feathers for the word. If they find it, they cover it with one of the prepared paper or felt feathers of the same color. The first child with all the colors covered is the winner. Have the children play this game without your help once they are familiar with it.

Illustrators

Explain to the children what the job of an illustrator is. Tell them that they can be illustrators too. Prepare books for them to illustrate by mimeographing pages with simple words or sentences with space for them to illustrate the words. Have them design covers and write "Illustrated by _____."

MATHEMATICS ACTIVITIES

Information, Please

Explain to the children how telephone operators give information to people who need help. Seat your class in rows for this game. Provide toy telephones for two of the children, a caller and an operator. The caller calls and asks the operator for a child in the group. Explain that they should ask using ordinal-number language, such as, "Give me the fourth child in the second row." The operator must tell who is being asked for. Give all the children a chance to be the operator or the caller.

Inchworms with Numbers

Provide circle patterns for the children to trace 10 circles attached in a row as an inchworm. Have them write the numbers 1–10 in the circles. Tell them to pretend the inchworm has to carry little Is on its back. Ask them to draw one I on the section labled "1," two on the section labeled "2," and so on.

Inchworm Counting

Prepare inchworms labeled with numbers you are teaching. Make one inchworm for each number. Give the children counters and ask them to put the correct number of spots on each inchworm.

SCIENCE ACTIVITIES

Insects

Teach about insects. Take the children on a nature walk to collect specimens. Bring the specimens into the classroom for observation. Provide books, pictures, filmstrips, and magnifying glasses for the children to use while studying the insects. Make an insect cage for the classroom by sewing shut a long cylinder of netting and inserting a circle of heavy cardboard at the top and the bottom. Tie the ends shut with yarn. Hang this from a light fixture in the room.

Insect Cage

MOVEMENT AND GAMES

Icicles

Have the children pretend to be icicles as they move about on the play area. Choose someone to be the sun. When the sun touches someone, he or she must "melt" and fall down, laying very still.

Inchworms

Play music and have the children move as inchworms on all fours. To move like an inchworm, they should move their arms first, making their bodies go down, down, down. Then their body arch comes up as they move their feet up, up, up.

ALPHABET APPETIZER

Individual Ice Creams

> ½ cup milk
> 1 teaspoon sugar
> 1 tablespoon powdered milk
> ¼ teaspoon flavoring (vanilla, mint, peppermint)

1. Have each child mix the ingredients in a metal can.
2. Cover the can with a piece of aluminum foil.
3. Set the can in a bowl with a lid that has a circle cut out of it to fit over the can.
4. Remove the lid. Fill the bowl around the can with crushed ice. Pour salt generously over the ice cubes. Put the lid back on.
5. Remove the foil from the can and stir the mixture, twist the can around, stir the mixture, and twist the can, repeating until ice cream forms.

Note: Pour a little water over the ice cubes to speed up the melting process.

metal can
bowl with lid
ice cubes and salt

Ice Cream Maker

ICE CREAM CONES

These ice cream cones are empty. Fill them up with scoops of ice cream. Look at the number on each cone to know how many scoops to put on the cone. Color in the flavors. On the back of this paper, draw a tall ice cream cone. Count how many scoops you put on and write that number on the cone.

COLOR THE INCHWORM

This inchworm needs color. Look at the numbers on it. Then look under the inchworm. The numbers stand for the color to make each part. Color in the parts. On the back of this paper, draw another colorful inchworm crawling in some grass.

1—red
2—yellow
3—blue
4—orange

Alphabet Activities reproducible page, copyright © 1983

Jj

ART ACTIVITIES

Jack-in-the-Boxes

Teach the children how to make an accordion fold. Have them fold a 1-by-11-inch strip of paper for the springy neck of the Jack-in-the-box. Let them cut out and decorate a colorful square box with lots of Js on it and a head for "Jolly Jack." Have them glue the head and the box to opposite ends of the folded strip.

Jungle Pictures

Have the children paint jungle pictures on large sheets of paper. Provide green, brown, yellow, and blue paint. Ask each child to tell about his or her picture when it has dried.

Jack-o'-Lanterns

Give each child eight 1½-by-18-inch strips of orange construction paper. Show the children how to glue these at the top and bottom to form a globe shape. Have them cut out eyes, nose, and mouth and glue them onto strips for the jack-o'-lantern's face. Glue a smaller strip into a ring for a handle. Have the children make their jack-o'-lanterns jiggle and jump by gently shaking them.

Junk Prints

Ask the children to collect junk from home. Show them how to print by dipping one of the ends of the pieces of junk into paint and pressing onto paper.

Provide several bright colors of paint and some junk such as spools, plastic silverware, corks, pencils, keys, blocks, game markers, combs, and the tops to containers of different shapes and sizes.

J Hooks

Give the children large sheets of paper. Have them design and paint or color large, jolly Js. Have them cut the Js out and hang other paper decorations on strings from the hooks of the letters.

READING AND WRITING READINESS

Jumping

On an old piece of plastic or a shower curtain, draw boxes with a permanent marker. In each box, print a letter you have introduced. As you call out a letter, have a child find the box and jump in it. Say a word and have a child jump in the box with the letter sound that word begins with.

Jellybean Js

Ask each child to cut out a large jellybean shape on his or her favorite color of paper. Ask the children to print Js on the jellybeans. Arrange the jellybeans in the shape of a giant J on the wall of the classroom during Jj week.

Jigsaw J

Cut out a large J from butcher paper. Divide and cut it into enough sections so that each child in the class will have a puzzle piece. Ask each child to decorate a section, and then put the pieces together as a class to form the J. (Draw a pattern of the puzzle before cutting it apart to make reassembling easier.)

Jingle

Have the children sit in a circle while you blindfold someone. Give another child a bell to ring. Have all the children hold their hands behind their backs so it will appear that they all are ringing a bell. Remove the blindfold and ask the child to guess who has the bell by listening to where the sound is coming from.

Jeans

Show the children how to cut out a pair of jeans from blue paper. Have them decorate the jeans with Js.

MATHEMATICS ACTIVITIES

Jars, Jars, and More Jars

Collect many jars of different sizes with lids. Open a size center in the classroom and have the children practice finding the correct lid for each jar. Let them practice size comparisons by arranging the jars in order from smallest to largest. Use jars to practice counting skills by taping numerals on them and having the children count beans, markers, or coins into them. Use them to teach measuring; for example, show how 2 pint jars of water equals 1 quart jar.

Jumpscotch

Place flashcards about a foot apart on the floor in a **J** shape. Have the children jump over the cards, calling out the number on each one. Use flashcards for any skill you are reviewing, such as number recognition, set configuration, shape identification, adding, or subtracting.

SCIENCE ACTIVITIES

Jungle

Teach the children about plants and animals found in the jungle. Provide many pictures, books, and filmstrips about life in the jungle. Be sure to include some material about the jaguar. Let the children draw pictures of life in a jungle. Help them write some simple sentences about jungles.

Jellyfish

Teach the children some interesting facts about the jellyfish. Let them draw jellyfish and label their pictures to take home.

MOVEMENT AND GAMES

J Movements

Ask the children to move by jiggling, jerking, jumping, jittering, and flying like jets.

Jumping Jacks

Teach the children to do the jumping-jack exercise. Introduce it slowly and increase the speed as the children become more proficient. Have them call out "**J**!" as they do each jumping jack.

Jog

Take some time each day of **Jj** week to jog with the children. Let the children call out "**J**!" to friends they meet while jogging. Keep track of how many minutes you jog each day, trying to increase your time.

Jump on the Jackrabbit

On the play area, chalk in a large shape of a jackrabbit. Ask the children to stand in a large circle around the jackrabbit. Call out children's names, telling them to jump on body parts of the jackrabbit. Make the game more difficult by adding *left* and *right* to the directions.

Jets

Ask the children to stand on a line at one end of the play area. Choose someone to be "It" and to call "Tower to jets, take off!" Have the players run to a line at the opposite end of the play area. When they reach the goal, have them call "Jets landing!" The first one to reach the goal becomes the new "It."

ALPHABET APPETIZER

Jellyrolls

First prepare this recipe for "Jiffy Jelly," a sugarless jelly, with your class:

> 1 12-ounce can of frozen apple juice concentrate, thawed
> ½ of a 1¾-ounce box of Slim Set
> slice of whole wheat bread for each child
> butter

Add the Slim Set to thawed juice. Heat to boiling. Simmer for one minute. Cool. Use this "Jiffy Jelly" to make the "jellyrolls."

Give each child a slice of whole wheat bread. Have the children cut off the crusts, then flatten the bread with a rolling pin or their hands. (Save the crusts of bread to feed birds.) Have them spread butter and some "Jiffy Jelly" on the bread, roll up the bread, and eat.

Note: Other spreads, such as peanut butter, cream cheese, honey, or applesauce, can be used.

JACK-IN-THE-BOXES

Help Jack find his way to each box below. Use a pencil to trace carefully over the lines to the box. On the back of your paper, write 10 capital Js and 10 lower-case Js. Draw a Jack-in-the-Box who is looking at them.

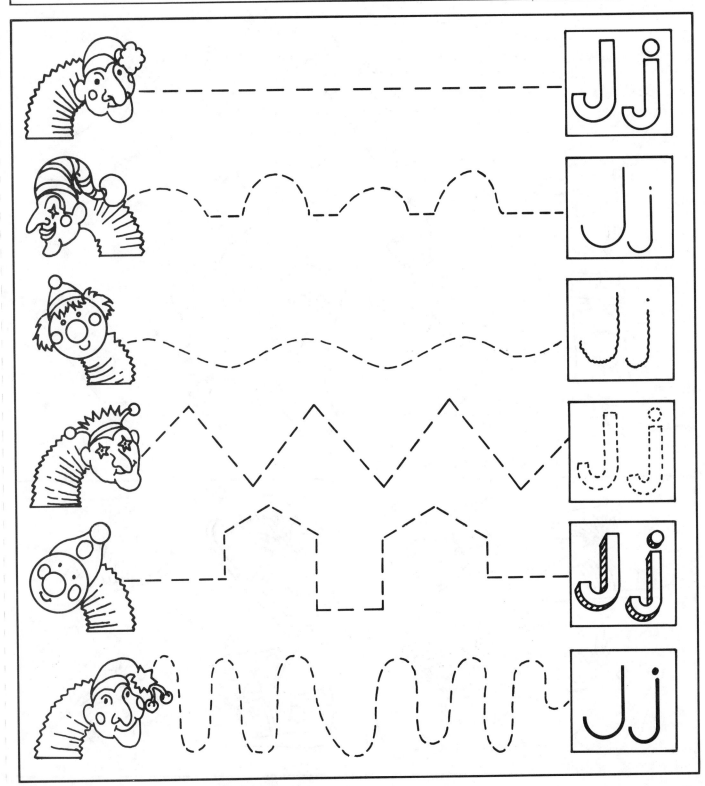

JOGGING SHOES

Cut out the jogging shoes at the bottom of the page. Glue each one onto the right sock by matching the correct capital and lower-case letters. On the back of this paper, draw a pair of special jogging shoes you would like to have. Write your favorite letter on them.

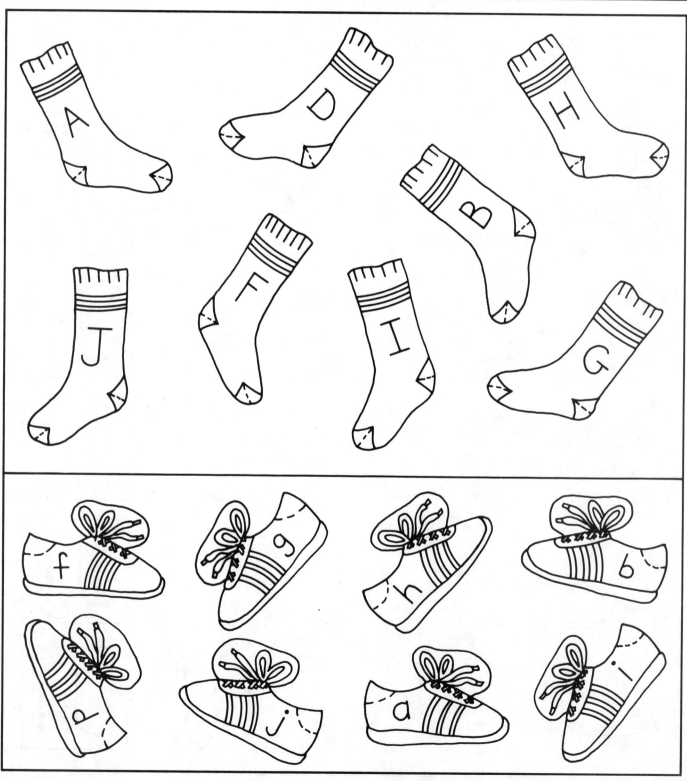

Alphabet Activities reproducible page, copyright © 1983

Kk

Kooky *K*s

Make a **K** for each child in the class to cut out and decorate in a "kooky" fashion. Arrange them into a display for **Kk** week.

Kittens

Read to the children a story about kittens. Talk with them about kittens. Ask the children who have kittens as pets to tell the others about what they look like and what they do. Give the children scratch paper and have them practice drawing kittens. Let them use the chalkboard to practice, too. Give them large sheets of paper to paint kittens. Write down something special that each child tells you about the kitten. Have them find all the **K**s in their recitations and draw kites around them.

Mama and Baby Kangaroos

Have the children draw a large kangaroo on a large sheet of brown paper and cut it out. Show them how to make a pocket for their kangaroos by cutting out a half circle and gluing all but the top edge of it to the kangaroo. Have the children draw and cut out a baby kangaroo to fit in the mother's pocket.

Kites

Invite a class of older children to come and help your children to make kites. When the weather permits, have the older and younger children go outdoors and fly the kites together. Stress the value of sharing and working cooperatively during this project.

Kitchens

Visit the kitchen in your school if one is available. Talk with the children about various things found in a kitchen. Have the children draw maps of their kitchens at home.

Keys

Provide an assortment of keys for the children to look at, talk about, sort, and count. After they have had time to do these things, have them pretend they have a special key to open anything in the world. Have them draw what they think the key would look like and tell you what it would open. Write down their words beside their drawings.

K Words

Provide some simple dictionaries or a word chart for the children to look at to help them write and illustrate **K** words. Prepare papers decorated with kites or keys for the children to write their words on.

Kickball

Divide the class into two teams. Have them sit in rows facing each other. In the space between the rows, mark off a diamond shape with tape. Explain to the children that the points of the diamond represent first base, second base, third base, and home plate. Show a letter flashcard to the child who is "up." If that person can name one word beginning with the letter, he or she kicks a ball and goes to first base. Those who name two words go to second base, those who name three words go to third base, and those who name four words kick a home run. Take turns drawing from children on each team. Keep score.

Sound of *K*

Explain to the children that **K** and hard **C** have the same sound. Let them practice making the sound out loud. On the chalkboard, write down some words that end in *ck* to show the children that sometimes these two sounds are used together, for example *pack, sack, peck, deck, sick, tick, sock, flock, tuck,* and *duck.*

Kernels of Corn

Bring in a bag of unpopped popcorn. Use kernels for counting, making sets, adding, subtracting, or forming tactile numerals and shapes.

K-Beanbag Toss

Make a large sheet of paper with circles drawn on it and tape it to the floor. Print a **K** and a numeral from 1 through 10 in each circle. Have the children take turns tossing beanbags into the circles. If they get a beanbag in a circle, they get the number of points indicated in the circle. Have the children keep track of their scores by counting out kernels of popcorn after each turn. At the end of the game, have everyone count their kernels to see who has the most.

Number Kites

Prepare an interactive bulletin board. Make kites and write different numerals on them, and attach the kites to the board with strings hanging down from each as tails. Have the children put the correct number of clip clothespins on each kite's tail to match the numeral written on the kite.

SCIENCE ACTIVITIES

Kernel Kapers

Have the children work in pairs or small groups to conduct this experiment. Tell the children to put several kernels of unpopped corn into a clear container of water. Put in an Alka Seltzer tablet and watch the kernels move up and down.

Kangaroos

Teach the children about kangaroos and their habits. Provide books, pictures, and filmstrips to help them learn. Have them draw pictures of kangaroos, and help them write something they learned about them.

Kittens

Let children with kittens for pets share them during **Kk** week. Ask them to bring the kittens to school to tell about them and to let the other children observe them. Make a large class book with a page for each kitten that visits the classroom. Have the children help you decide what to write and draw.

MOVEMENT AND GAMES

Movements for *K*

Ask the children to kick while doing the movements of walking, running, and hopping. Have them pretend to be jumping kangaroos and crawling kittens and greet each other with the sound of **K** as they meet.

King Away

Choose one child to leave the room. Choose someone else to pretend to be a king away on a trip for the kingdom. Have that child hide in a closet or under a blanket. Have the first child return to the room and try to decide who the king is. Choose more than one king at a time to make the game more difficult.

Kicking Practice

Divide the class into two groups and have them stand on lines opposite each other. Direct the children to kick balls back and forth to each other.

Keep It Up

Divide the class into teams of four or five children. Give each team a blown-up balloon with **K**s printed on it. When you call out "K!" they must hit the balloon up, trying not to let it fall to the ground. If a balloon touches the ground, the team must stop playing and sit down. The last team with its balloon up is the winner. Let them play this game several times. Substitute balls or beanbags for balloons.

ALPHABET APPETIZER

Kangaroo Pockets

Provide a half slice of pita, or pocket, bread for each child. Show the children how to butter it and put a slice of cheese into it. Have them wrap it up in aluminum foil and hold a hot iron on each side until the cheese melts. (If pita bread is not available, use a regular bread that is thinly sliced.)

KEY
WORDS

Look at the word in the key at the left of each line. Find the other word in the line that is exactly like the word in the key, and draw a circle around it.

key   key   ket   keep

kite   kit   kite   kits

kid   king   kon   kid

kind   kind   kiss   king

kick   kit   kick   kangaroo

kitten   kitchen   king   kitten

kit   ket   kit   keep

kangaroo   kitchen   kindergarten   kangaroo

keep   keep   king   keel

king   king   kind   kiss

KITES AND COLORS

Read the color word on each kite and color the kites. Trace the **K** on each kite with a black crayon. On the back of this paper, design a kite you would like to fly.

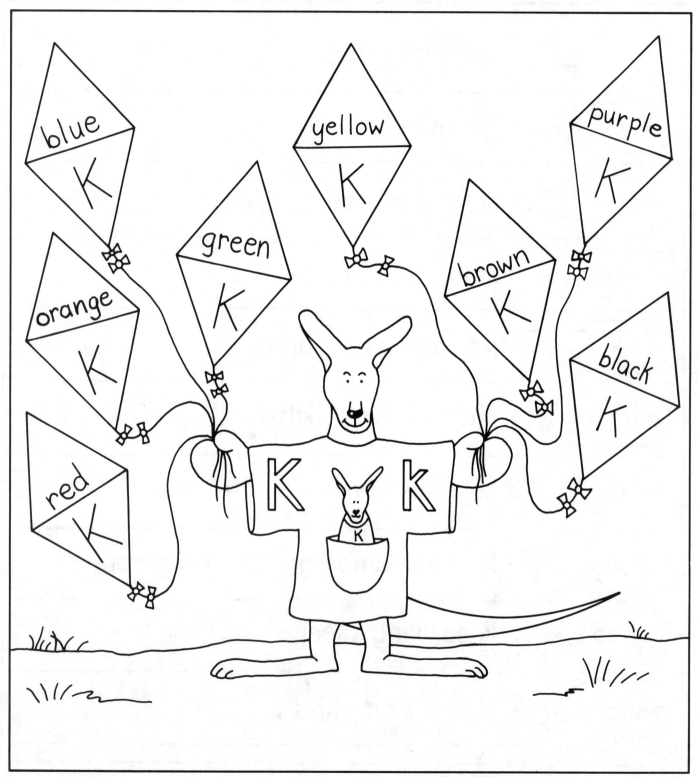

Ll

ART ACTIVITIES

Leaf Lanterns

Have the children collect interesting leaves and iron them between doubled sheets of waxed paper (about 18 inches when doubled). Show them how to staple a 4-by-18-inch strip of colored construction paper to the top and bottom of the waxed paper, folded the long way. Have the children roll this flat piece into a cylinder and staple it. Let them cut out fancy handles to staple onto the lanterns.

Leaping Leprechauns

Have the children cut out the following parts from different shades of green paper to make a small leprechaun: head, arms, legs, body, boots, mittens, and hat. Instruct them to glue head to body, hat to head, boots to legs, and mittens to arms. With brass fasteners, show them how to attach arms and legs to the body so that they can make their leprechauns leap by moving the arms and legs.

Ladders

Give each child three drinking straws. Show the children how to glue two straws onto a sheet of paper for the sides of a ladder. The other straw should be cut into equal-sized pieces for the rungs of the ladder and glued between the sides. Have the children draw a creature whose name begins with the letter **L** to stand at the bottom of the ladder.

Lacy *L*s

Ask parents to send in pieces of lace they no longer want. Have the children cut out a capital and a lower-case **L** and glue the lace pieces onto them. Put them in a display labeled "Lacy **L**s."

Large, Laughing *L*s

Draw large **L**s for each child in the class. Have the children cut out their letters and decorate them, mak-ing them laughing and happy. Ask the children to make up some silly stories about why the **L**s are laughing.

Lost Leaves

Ask the children to "hide" some leaves under a sheet of construction paper. Have them find the leaves by rubbing over the paper with the sides of crayons. Provide some cut-out **L**s to put under the papers with the leaves.

READING AND WRITING READINESS

Look for Me

Have the children sit around you as you hold an object beginning with the letter **L**. Ask one child at a time to look around the room for something bigger, smaller, rounder, shorter, brighter, lighter, heavier, or more colorful than the object you are holding.

Listening Center

Set up a listening center during **Ll** week. Stress to the children the importance of being quiet and still while others are listening. Record a story with an **L** theme for them to listen to, or use commercially prepared books with records or tapes.

Lacing Cards

Provide lacing cards for the children to manipulate. Make a set of large letters with holes for lacing. Have the children share their lacing work with someone else before undoing it.

Love Letter

Have the children make simple love letters for people who are special to them. Have them tuck it into a 4-inch piece of cardboard tubing (from paper towels or wrapping paper). Show them how to cover the tube with paper that is several inches longer than the tube. Let them fringe the ends and tie them with yarn. Encourage them to decorate the outside.

Sound of *L*

Teach the children the sound of the letter **L**. Have them feel how the tongue touches the roof of the mouth and then goes down. Let them practice making the sound out loud. Have them repeat words after you and decide if they begin with the sound of **L**.

MATHEMATICS ACTIVITIES

Listening to Numbers

Work with small groups of children to play this number game. Say three numbers and tell a child to repeat what you have said. Do this both orally and as a written exercise. After using three-number combinations, increase to four and five numbers at a time.

License Plate Game

Prepare a set of large cardboard license plates with numerals printed on them. Make a set of smaller duplicates and put them into a box. Have the children choose a small license plate and match it to a larger one. Increase the difficulty of this game by adding more numerals to each plate.

Ladybug Numbers

Cut out a set of ladybugs without spots. Cut out black circles for spots. Write a numeral on each ladybug. Have the children decorate the ladybugs with the correct number of spots.

SCIENCE ACTIVITIES

Leaves Grow

If you are studying the letter **L** in the spring, try this project. Choose a tree for your children to use. Once a week, let each child pick a leaf off the tree to iron between waxed paper. Have them indicate the date on each leaf, then collect the leaves. After several weeks, hand back all the leaves for the children to see how they grew. Have them put the leaves in order in a booklet or on a chart to take home.

Light and Dark

Talk with the children about light. Make a list of all its sources. Turn on an overhead projector and have the children take turns putting their hands over the screen to see the shadows they can make. Bring several flashlights to school for the children to use to move light around. Have them do a "light dance" to music using the flashlights.

Litter

Discuss with the children what litter is and where it comes from. Ask each child to bring a paper sack to school to pick up litter on the school grounds. Caution the children not to pick up broken glass and sharp objects by themselves.

MOVEMENT AND GAMES

Leaping

Ask the children to move about the play area with leaping movements. Have them call out "L!" as they land.

Ladder Activities

During **Ll** week, provide one or more ladders for use in the gym or play area. Have the children perform the following actions: walk along the sides of the ladder, between the rungs of the ladder, and on the rungs of the ladder; crawl between the rungs and along the sides; go backward on the ladder, repeating the previous movements; and crawl on the ladder when it is raised up by mats with more mats placed beneath it.

Leader Ball

Divide the class into groups of four or five, and choose one child in each group to be the leader. Have each leader stand facing a line of the children in that group. Tell the leader to throw the ball to each child in the group, who then must return it. When players miss, they go to the end of the line and the next player becomes the leader. Have the groups practice skills of catching, throwing, bouncing, and rolling.

ALPHABET APPETIZER

Lots of Layers

Provide each child with a clear plastic tumbler to make this nutritious and delicious dish. Have the children layer in the cup ¼ cup milk or yogurt, chopped fruit, such as bananas, peaches, pineapple, cooked apples, oranges, or pears, and ¼ cup granola or another nutritious cereal. Have them continue layering with a different chopped fruit, 1 tablespoon wheat germ, and a few raisins or nuts or both.

LADYBUG LADDER

Look at the ladybugs at the right. Cut them out and glue them next to the number on the ladder that tells how many spots they have. On the back of this paper, make a ladder with five rungs. Draw something that begins with **L** on each rung.

Give this ladybug ten 10 spots.

Give this ladybug one 1 spot.

Trace the **L**s.

LOOK BOOK

Make a book to read! Cut out the pages below. Staple them together and decorate the cover and pages. Write your name on the blank line on the cover. Read!

My Lok Book

by _____

Look at the lion.

L

Look at the letter **L**.

Look at the leaf.

Look at the ladybugs.

Look at the little lamb.

50

Alphabet Activities reproducible page, copyright © 1983

Mm

ART ACTIVITIES

Mustaches

Have the children draw and color a large face picture. When they have filled in the space well with color, have them cut out a paper mustache, curl the ends, and glue it onto their picture. Ask them to think of **M** names for their faces.

Moon Creatures

Give each child a sheet of white paper. Have them close their eyes and tear out any big funny shape. When they open their eyes, ask them to imagine that their shape is the beginning of a moon creature. Let them add arms, legs, antennae, and other features by cutting out and gluing on colored-paper parts.

Monkeys

Show the children how to make a monkey by cutting out circles for the head and body. Demonstrate how to accordion-fold long, inch-wide strips of paper for the arms and legs. Have the children glue the parts together and add facial features, a tail, big ears, and a hat with an **M** on it.

Masks

Provide for each child a paper sack to fit over the head. Help them cut out holes for the eyes, nose, and mouth. Give them a choice of materials to decorate their masks. Divide the class into small groups to make up little plays. Let them perform for each other.

Mad *M* Machines

Have the children design machines, using paper and attaching working parts with brass fasteners, paper clips, and glue. Let them cut out and glue on or draw on buttons, knobs, and handles to make the machines "work." Encourage them to think of things that begin with the letter **M** that their machines might do, such as make moons or money or manage monkeys.

Me Books

Have the children make books about themselves. Provide blank pages for the books and colored paper for front and back covers. Have them make one page with a picture of themselves with their names, and a page each for their house, their family, favorite foods, friends, and things they like to do. Help them with language if they want to write words in the books.

What's Missing?

Bring to class some things that have a part missing, or draw pictures of them. Have the children take turns examining them and telling what is missing. Some ideas of things to bring are a sock without a toe, a shoe without a lace, a shirt without a sleeve, a blouse without buttons, a pair of pants without a leg, a pencil without lead, and a fork with missing prongs.

Magazines for **M**

Ask the children to look through magazines for **M**s and things beginning with the sound of **M**. Have them glue or paste these things on a small duplicated mouse you prepare or on a large class mouse for the wall.

Macaroni *M*s

Have the children print a large capital and a lower-case **M** on a sheet of paper. Show them how to glue macaroni onto the lines. When the macaroni is dry, have the children carefully color it with fine-line markers.

M Mobiles

Give each child a strip of cardboard for the base of a mobile. Have them design and cut out a capital and a lower-case **M** and pictures of things beginning with the sound of **M**. Show them how to tie these paper objects to the cardboard strip with yarn or string of varying lengths. Hang the mobiles from the light fixtures in your room.

Matching

Give the children experience in matching by finding things that are exactly the same. Provide a variety of things to match, such as wordcards, lettercards, numbercards, shapes, and material swatches. Provide materials of varying degrees of difficulty.

MATHEMATICS ACTIVITIES

Mailperson

Prepare a bulletin board for the children to use. Make houses with five-digit numerals on them. Attach an envelope to each house for mail to be delivered. For letters, use cards that will fit easily into the envelopes. Write the numbers of the houses on the cards, making more than one letter for each house. Have the children take turns being the mailperson.

Money

Set up a center in the room for the children to learn about money. Put a few of each of these coins in the center—nickel, dime, penny, and quarter. Prepare some simple games in which the children have to sort the money according to its value. Begin with this puzzle game. Make circles and cut them apart in different patterns. On one half of the circle, write the value of the coin, and on the other half put a small picture of the coin. If the children are successful in their matching, all the puzzle pieces will fit. Provide a toy cash register as well as a bank game in which the children count coins into jars labeled 1–20.

SCIENCE ACTIVITIES

Melting

Provide clear plastic cups for the children to decorate using fine-line markers. Have them write their names on their cups. Place the cups on a cookie sheet in a 350° oven for several minutes. Watch them carefully and take them out just after they change their shape. Have the children use them as vases and as containers for their collections of things.

Make a Magnet

Demonstrate to the children how to make a magnet by wrapping insulated copper wire around a large stove bolt or a screwdriver. Connect the ends of the wire to a dry-cell battery. Provide objects for the children to test with this magnet. Have the children make a chart, drawing pictures of the things the magnet held and did not hold.

Moon

Teach the children some interesting facts about the moon. Show them filmstrips and pictures. Read them some simple stories. Talk with them about spaceships and astronauts who have gone to the moon. Ask each child to tell you something special he or she learned about the moon, and write their words on a moon mural.

MOVEMENT AND GAMES

Mirrors

Explain to the children that they are to mirror whatever action you perform. This should be a quiet activity with the children watching carefully. Do all kinds of motions, such as raising arms, bending over, smiling, and tilting the head. As a variation, divide the class into pairs and let the children be each other's mirrors.

Marching

Play some rousing music for the children. Vary the tempo so the children march slowly, quickly, with high steps, on tiptoe, with heavy feet, with light feet, in a silly way, and so forth.

Mousetrap

Have the children form a circle. Choose two children to make a bridge or trap by holding their arms together above their heads. Play music as the children form a line and walk under the mousetrap. When the music stops, the child under the mousetrap is "caught." Each time two children are caught, they form a new trap beside the beginning trap for the rest of the class to pass under. Play the game until everyone is part of a trap.

ALPHABET APPETIZER

Monster Mash

Provide each child with a small bowl and a sturdy fork. Have them mix and mash a half or third of a banana, ¼ cup applesauce, 1 teaspoon honey, and 1 teaspoon peanut butter. Have them sprinkle the top of the Monster Mash with cinnamon, coconut, or raisins.

SPELL THE
M WORDS

Use a dictionary or a word chart to find the words for these **M** pictures. Write the letters on the lines by the pictures. On the back of this paper, write and illustrate your five favorite **M** words.

MISSING MITTENS

Cut out the mittens on the bottom of this page. Glue each of them onto the mouse that has a mitten with the same pattern. Trace over the **M**s on each mouse. On the back of this paper, make a marvelous pair of mittens you would like to have. Be sure to draw **M**s on them.

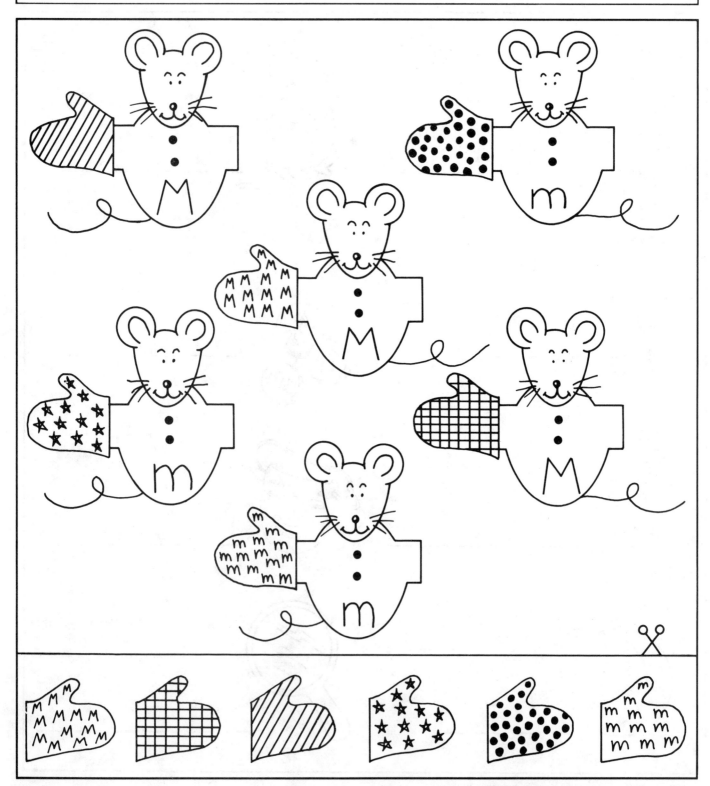

Alphabet Activities reproducible page, copyright © 1983

ART ACTIVITIES

Noodle Art

Bring an assortment of noodles for the art center. Have the children glue noodles onto colorful paper to design a picture. When the noodles are dry, have the children add color to the pictures.

Name Art

Write each child's name with a black marker on a sheet of white construction paper. Have the children "rainbow" around each letter, using each of the eight basic colors. Have them cut out their name after the last color has been added. Let the children rainbow-write other words they know.

Nail Pictures

Ask the children to create a design on a small block of wood by pounding in nails with large heads. After they have pounded in their pictures, have them color the tops of the nails with markers and add other decorative touches to the wood. Nails should not be pounded all the way down, but left to protrude about ½ inch out of the wood.

Nests

Give each child a small paper plate. Have the children tear newspaper strips to "build" a nest on the plate, gluing it down around the edges. Have them cut out a bird to sit in the nest.

Net Pictures

Give each child a small piece of nylon netting. Have the children use their imaginations to create a picture around the netting, attaching it to the paper in any way they choose to fit the picture they make.

READING AND WRITING READINESS

No and Not

Teach *no* and *not* to the children during **Nn** week. Have the children read and write simple sentences with these words.

Noisy Books

Prepare an empty book for each child. Have the children look in magazines and newspapers for pictures of things that make noise. Have them glue the pictures onto the pages of the book. Ask the children to number the pages in the book when they are finished.

Near and Far

Have one child face a wall in the classroom. Have two other children stand behind the one facing the wall—one near, and the other farther away. Have the two children who are standing say something such as "Newts are nice; where am I standing?" The first child tries to guess if the one talking is near or far. Let the child also try to identify the speaker.

Name Notebooks

Provide many small sheets of paper for the children to make name notebooks. Have the children take one sheet for each name they write. Staple all their names together and give them paper to decorate for a cover. Let the children practice reading the names in their name notebooks. To help the children begin this activity, prepare a flashcard for each child in the room with their name and a small picture of them beside it.

Name Puzzles

Prepare each child's name with the letters cut apart like a puzzle. Put each name in a different envelope labeled with the name. Have the children solve each other's names.

Needle an *N*

Cut up pieces of old sheeting or other scrap material. With a marker, print a capital and a lower-case **N** on each. Thread and knot needles for the children to sew over the lines of the **N**s.

MATHEMATICS ACTIVITIES

Number Catch

Have the children form a circle, counting off so that everyone has a number. Write the numerals on paper, and pin or tape them to the children to help them remember their numbers. Stand in the center of the cricle with a ball. Throw the ball in the air and call commands such as "The number before four" or "The number after seven." The person addressed must catch the ball. Ask the children to exchange numbers during the game.

Ns for Sale

Prepare a stack of number cards 1–20. Divide the class into two teams. Seat the children from one team in a half circle facing the wall. Name them the buyers. Seat the other team, the sellers, in a line. Have one child from the "seller" team take a card from the stack of number cards, place the card on the floor, and say, "Ns for sale, will you buy my Ns?" Have the child use a stick to tap out the number from the card. Have the first child in the half circle answer, "Yes, I'll buy six *(or whatever number was tapped)* Ns." If the children answering are right, they exchange places with the sellers. Continue the game until everyone has had a turn as a seller.

Number Nine

Work with the children on learning to write the numeral nine and build sets of that number. Help them learn to identify the set configuration of three rows of three as nine.

SCIENCE ACTIVITIES

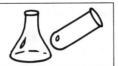

Nature

Take the class on a nature walk. Look at trees, plants, flowers, weeds, insects, birds, rocks, and leaves. When the children return to the classroom, have them paint or draw large pictures depicting the things they observed in nature.

Nose Activities

Prepare a set of small bottles with different smells. Put a drop of each fragrance on cotton balls. Have the children identify the odors through the sense of smell. Make a set of picture cards representing the smells; have the children match each picture with the correct bottle.

Night Animals

Teach the children some facts about animals that are awake at night. Give the children sheets of black paper. Have them paint pictures of night animals. Have the children tell you something about their pictures, and write it down. Have the children find and circle the Ns in their recitations.

MOVEMENT AND GAMES

Nightingales and Nests

Have the children pretend they are nightingales flying around the play area, singing the letter N. When you call "Nest!" have them pretend to sit in a nest wherever they are.

Necktie Relay

Divide the class into two teams. Provide a necktie for each team. The first player in each line ties the necktie around his or her neck and shakes hands with the next person in the line. The second players must untie it, tie it onto themselves, shake hands with the third persons in line, and so on. The first team to have everyone finished tying wins.

ALPHABET APPETIZER

Nibblers

Provide a cup and a teaspoon for each child. Have them scoop a spoonful of some of the following foods into their cups: granola, peanuts, wheat germ, raisins, coconut, dry-cereal bits, sunflower seeds, pretzel pieces, sesame sticks, dried fruit pieces, and walnuts. Have the children stir and nibble.

NAMES, NAMES!

Print your first and last name on the line below. Get a sheet of newspaper. Find all the letters in your name and cut them out. Glue the letters under the newt in the same order as they appear in your name. On the back of this paper, practice making nifty **N**s.

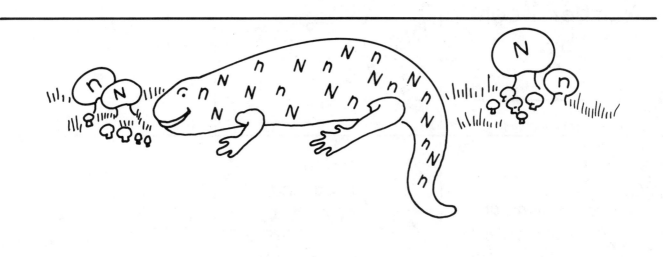

NUMBER POEMS

Cut out each of the squares below. Put them together to make a number book. Trace over the numbers and learn the poem for each one. Practice writing your numbers with the poems.

My Number Book by _____	Around we go!	One is fun!
Around and back on a railroad track!	Around a tree and around a tree, that's the way to make a three.	Down and over and down some more, that's the way to make a four.
Fat old five goes down, around. Put a hat on top.	Roll a hoop and make a loop.	Across the sky and down from heaven, that's the way to make a seven.
We make an "S" but do not wait, go back up and close the gate.	A hoop and a line, that makes a nine.	The End

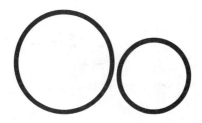

Oo

Torn Os

Give each child an 8-inch square of orange paper. Show the children how to tear around the outside edge of the paper, making a round shape. Have them carefully tear out the center of the circle. Form a large class **O** for a display during **Oo** week.

O Button Pictures

Give each child a handful of buttons or **O**-shaped cereal to glue to a paper in the shape of an **O**. Encourage the children to use their imaginations to create a picture around the **O**, using it as part of the design.

Octopus in the Ocean

Provide a margarine tub for each child to use as the body of an octopus. Have them cut out eight legs and tape or glue them to the lid of the margarine container. Direct the children to fit the lid on the upside-down tub. Have them use markers to add eyes, mouths, and other features.

 READING AND WRITING READINESS

Open House

Hold an open house during **Oo** week. Invite parents and friends of the children. Serve oatmeal cookies or another **O** treat. Have the guests sign a special Open House Book you have prepared. Read the names to the children the next day and place the book in your class library.

Oops!

Ask the children to sit in a circle. Make up imaginary situations and have the children tell what they would

say or do if these things really happened to them. Some examples are if a cow said "Bow-wow," if a 5 talked to you, if you tripped over a kangaroo, if you met a purple elephant, if you saw someone with four eyes, if you turned into an apple, if an octopus rang your doorbell, if an otter and an owl danced on your lawn, and if an ostrich came for dinner. Write down their narratives and have them color in all the **O**s.

Octopus Stories

Ask the children to draw pictures of an octopus having adventures in the ocean. Have them tell you a story, and write it down for them. Have them find the **O**s in their narratives and trace them with an orange crayon.

Making Os

Teach the children the correct formation of the letter **O**. Explain that it is the beginning of many other letters. Have the children try to write the other letters that have the shape of **O** in them. Provide an alphabet chart for them to look at for this activity.

Office

Locate an old typewriter or two for your room, and place them on desks in a corner for a pretend office. Put in a file box, pens, paper clips, markers, rubber bands, and play telephones. Try to put the office near a chalkboard so the children can write messages as they play. Keep the typewriter in your writing center for the entire year, if possible, for the children to type their names, the ABCs, and other words.

 MATHEMATICS ACTIVITIES

Ordering Numbers

Have the children put sets of numbers in order. Provide a variety of sets, such as numbers on flashcards, blocks, bottle caps, playing cards, beads, and puzzles.

O Number Book

Show the children how to make a special counting book for **Oo** week. Provide 10 small sheets of paper stapled together and a container of ring macaroni for **O**s for each child. On the first page, have them write 1 and glue on one macaroni. On the second page, have them write 2 and glue two, and so on. Let them make covers for their books if desired.

Old Octopus

Prepare a deck of cards, making a picture of an old octopus on one card and using two cards for each number you are studying. Pass out the cards to a small group of children so that everyone has the same amount. Have the children hold their cards out in front of them in a fan formation. Have them take turns drawing one card at a time from each other. When they have a match, have them put the pair down. At the end of the game, the person left holding the old octopus is the loser. You can make cardholders for the children by putting two margarine lids together top-to-top and fastening them with a brass fastener. The children can slip the cards between the lids and hold them easily.

SCIENCE ACTIVITIES

Oceans

Provide books, pictures, and filmstrips of oceans and ocean life. Make a game of pictures for the children to sort according to "lives in the ocean" and "does not live in the ocean." Provide water colors for the children to paint scenes from the ocean.

Olympic Weight Lifters

Provide each child with a bean that has been soaked in water overnight and a small paper cup with some dirt. Have them press the seed into the dirt. Give each child a penny to place over the spot where the seed is pressed in. Encourage the children to care for their plant by watering it. Have them watch to see whose seed lifts and tips the penny over first.

MOVEMENT AND GAMES

Over Heads

Have the children form two lines, with everyone in each line facing forward. Give a beanbag to the first child in each line and call the signal "O!" Have the children pass the beanbag over their heads toward the back. Have the last child in the line carry the beanbag back to the front. A ball or box may be used in place of the beanbag.

O Movements

Play music and let the children move like ostriches, owls, octopuses, oxen, and otters. Let them make the sound of **O** as they move.

O on the Floor

Tape or chalk a large **O** on the floor or playground. Direct the children to use the lines to walk, run, and skip on, and crawl, crab walk, and bear walk around. Encourage the children to think of other movements that would be fun to do using the **O**.

Body Os

Have the children roll their bodies into the shape of the letter **O**. Pair the children up and have each pair lay on the floor to form the letter. Have all the children lay down on the floor to form a class **O**. When the letter is formed, have them all say the short sound of **O** together.

ALPHABET APPETIZER

Os in Orange Juice

Have each child measure ½ cup orange juice into a paper cup. Provide each child with a third of a banana to cut into rings. Show the children how to poke out a hole in the center of each banana ring with a straw, forming **O**s. Have the children drop the banana **O**s into the juice. Give each child a few pretzel sticks with which to fish out the **O**s as they eat and drink.

OH-OH'S OVALS

Help Oh-Oh Octopus find the right ovals for each arm by matching the color words. Cut out the ovals at the bottom of the paper. Glue them to the matching arms. Color the ovals. Fill the ocean around Oh-Oh with **O**s. On the back of this paper, color an octopus holding an **O** on each arm. Make each **O** a different color.

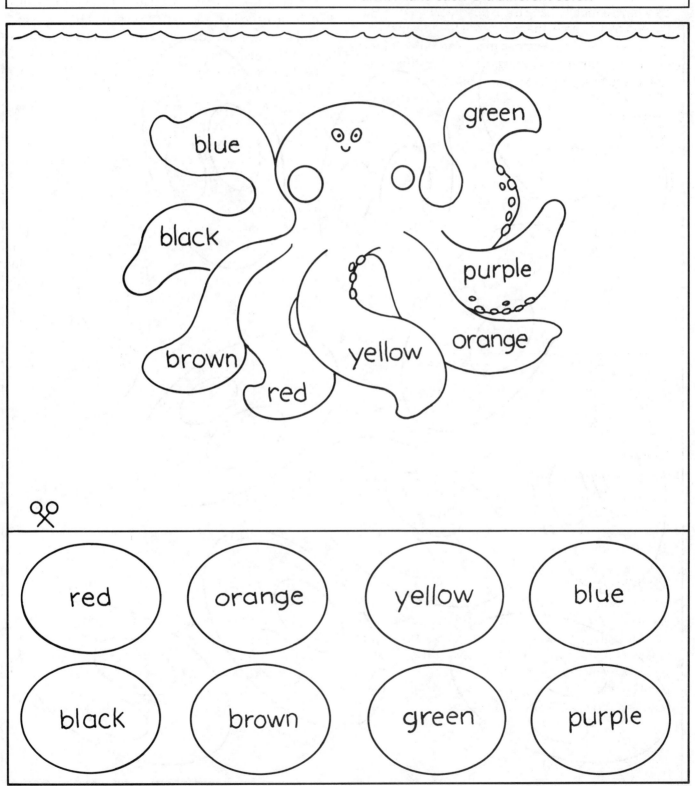

61

AN O OF OVALS

Color and cut out these ovals. Put them together to make the letter **O**. Put the oval pieces in an envelope so you can make the **O** again, or glue the ovals down on a sheet of paper. Trace over the **O**s.

Pp

ART ACTIVITIES

Pudding Painting

Mix up several batches of instant pudding for the children to finger-paint with. Have them make pictures of **P**s and things beginning with the letter **P**.

Potato Porcupines

Provide toothpicks and potatoes for the children to create porcupines. Have the children stick toothpicks into the body for legs and quills. Show the children how to add eyes by inserting tacks in paper circles.

Polka-Dotted *P*s

Prepare a **P** for each child to cut out and decorate with polka dots. Form them into a large capital and a lower-case **P** for a display during **Pp** week.

Pea Creations

Give each child a handful of frozen peas and some toothpicks for a pea creation. Show them how to build by sticking the toothpick ends into peas, much the same as Tinkertoys. Toothpicks can be broken into smaller pieces. Try to use the peas while they are still frozen. Let the children taste a few peas as they work.

Pumpkin Puzzle

Make a large pumpkin on orange paper. Divide it with a black marker into enough puzzle pieces for each child to have one. Draw a pattern of the puzzle before cutting it up. Give each child a section of the puzzle to decorate and print **P**s on. When everyone is finished, assemble the pumpkin. Glue it to a large paper and hang it up for everyone to see.

Pussy Willow Pictures

Have the children draw a branch on a sheet of construction paper. Show the children how to pull apart cotton balls and roll them into tiny balls. Have them glue their pussy willows onto the branch.

READING AND WRITING READINESS

Peg Boards

Supply the children with peg boards and lots of pegs with which to create pictures, letters, shapes, and designs. Prepare some patterns for them to copy. Encourage everyone to form **P**s.

People Books

Have the children use magazines to find and cut out pictures of people. Have them look for all kinds of people—babies, children, adults, older people. Provide paper for the children to paste the pictures on. Prepare a word chart so they can label their pictures. Staple all the pages into books, and have each child make a cover saying "My People Book by
_____."

Pencils

Teach the children to hold pencils correctly. Ask them to draw a special **P** picture using their pencils.

Police Officer

Have the children sit in a circle. Play the part of a parent. Choose someone to be the police officer. Tell the officer that your child is lost, and describe your child to him or her. From your description, the officer must identify who your child is. Give all the children a turn to be a parent or a police officer.

MATHEMATICS ACTIVITIES

Patterning

Work with the children on making patterns. Use objects such as silverware, blocks, beads, and pegs. Begin with simple patterns, such as something red, something blue, something red, and something blue. As the children become more proficient, increase the difficulty of the task by introducing patterns involving more than just color—for example, red square, blue circle, green triangle, red square, blue circle, green triangle, and so on. Ask the children to continue the patterns. Have the children make patterns for each other to copy.

Pincushion Game

Have small groups of children use this game for making sets and counting. Prepare pincushions by gluing pieces of sponge to cardboard and writing a numeral and set connotation between 1 and 10 on each. Provide straight pins with colored heads for the children to count and stick into the pincushions.

Pennies

Teach the children to recognize a penny and learn its value. Place a container of pennies in the math center for children to count and make sets with and to use for simple arithmetic.

SCIENCE ACTIVITIES

Pet Parade

Talk with the children about their pets. Set aside a special day during **Pp** week for a pet parade. Have parents help bring in the pets for a designated amount of time. Let each child have a chance to show and talk about his or her pet. Outdoors or in a large area such as a gym, play music as the children walk around with their pets. Let children who do not have pets help those that do. Invite another class to the parade.

Potato Planters

Provide each child with a potato. Help the children hollow out the inside of the potato leaving a strong wall. Let the child decorate the outside of the potato with buttons, pipe cleaners, yarn, and such. Have them fill the potato with soil and sprinkle grass seed over it. Have the children water the seeds and watch them grow.

Pushy Pepper

Have the children work in pairs for this experiment. Give them a small dish to fill with water. Have them sprinkle some black pepper gently over the top. Then

have them place a small piece of soap into the water and watch how the pepper moves away from it. (The pepper moves away as the soap dissolves, giving off an oily film that the pepper can't penetrate.)

MOVEMENT AND GAMES

Movement as *P* Things

Have the children move to music as pigs, porcupines, popping popcorn, rolling potatoes, pieces of paper being flipped and turned, and pussy willows in the wind.

Popping Popcorn

Ask children to spread out on the play area. When you blow your whistle once, have them become popping popcorn by hopping about making the sound of **P**. When you blow the whistle twice, they must sit or lay down and be completely still until you blow your whistle again.

Pass the Potato

Have the children sit in a circle. Let them pass a ball around by tossing it as you play music. When the music stops, whoever is holding the ball is "out." Direct each child who is "out" to another activity such as jumping rope, tumbling, or playing catch.

ALPHABET APPETIZER

Peanut Butter

Have the children help shell enough peanuts to fill 2 cups. Put 2 tablespoons of salad oil into a blender. Add the peanuts gradually, blending until smooth. Serve on bread, on crackers, or in celery.

PUZZLE TIME

Cut out the puzzle pieces and the sentence strips below. Glue the puzzles together on another sheet of paper, and glue the correct sentence under each one.

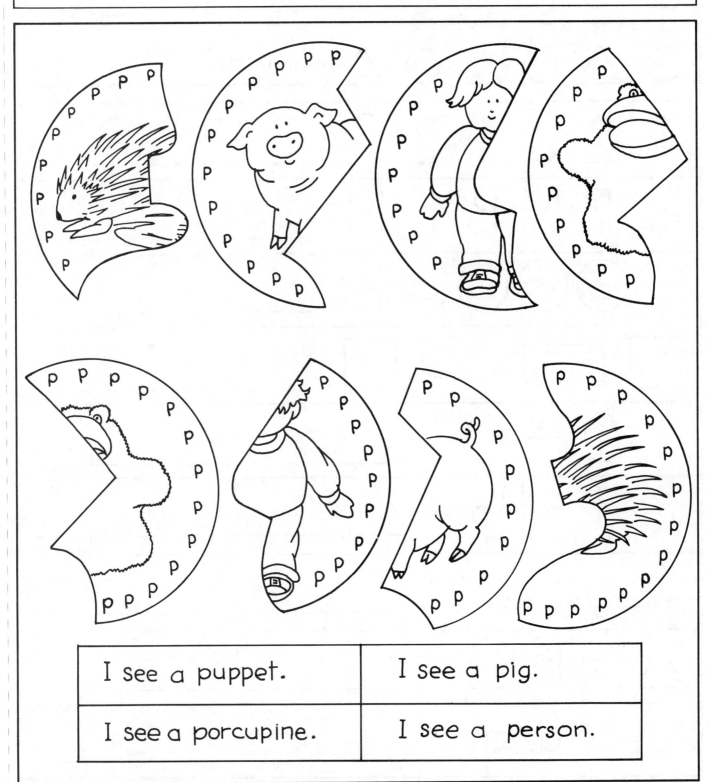

I see a puppet.	I see a pig.
I see a porcupine.	I see a person.

PATTERNS FOR YOU

Look at the pattern next to each number below. Using a pencil, continue each pattern in the spaces at the right. On the back of this paper, make up five patterns of your own. Let a friend continue them. Color your patterns when you are finished.

○ △ △ ○ △ ○ ○ △ _ _ _ _ _ _ _ _ _

1 2 3 1 2 3 _ _ _ _ _ _ _ _ _

B F M B F M _ _ _ _ _ _ _ _

☺ ☺ ☹ ☺ ☺ ☹ _ _ _ _ _ _ _ _

□ ▭ ⬭ □ _ _ _ _ _ _ _ _

+ ○ + ○ _ _ _ _ _ _ _ _

P p P p P p _ _ _ _ _ _ _ _

•• — — •• — _ _ _ _ _ _ _ _ _ _

△ ✕ P □ _ _ _ _ _ _ _ _ _

b p d q _ _ _ _ _ _ _ _

ART ACTIVITIES

Queens with Crowns

Have the children paint pictures of queens wearing crowns with **Q**s on them.

Q-tip Pictures

Give each child a few Q-tips to glue onto a sheet of paper and make a picture around.

A *Q* From Qs

Have the children lightly pencil a **Q** on a sheet of paper. Show them how to fill in the lines of the **Q** by printing little **Q**s very close together. Encourage them to make a lower-case **Q** as well.

Quackers

Provide each child with two sections of a styrofoam egg carton. The top section becomes the head, and the bottom the body, of a duck. Ask them to create a "quacker" by cutting out and gluing on paper wings, a beak, feet, and eyes. Provide a time for the children to tell something about their quackers.

READING AND WRITING READINESS

Quiet Center

During **Qq** week, set aside a special area of the classroom for quiet activities such as reading books, looking at pictures, drawing, or writing. Place a pretty rug, some pillows, and a rocking chair in the quiet center for the children's comfort. Include a record player or tape recorder with a set of earphones for the children to listen to stories and music.

Questions

Teach the children what a question is. Let them practice making up questions. Make up a set of sentences in which some are questions and some are not. Give each child a question mark and a period on little cards you have prepared. When you ask a question, have them hold up the question mark; otherwise, they should hold up the period.

Quilt

The children will each need a set of crayons and a copy of the worksheet on page 70 for this lesson. For each numbered square on the worksheet, dictate a direction:

1. Write the word *go* and make a green ball.
2. Write the numeral 10 and draw ten small circles in the box.
3. Draw three red circles. Color them in.
4. Draw four blue triangles. Put a dot in the center of each one.
5. Draw two green rectangles. Make a snake inside each of them.
6. Draw a picture of something you like to eat. Print the first letter of that word.
7. Make a yellow square. Color it in.
8. Color this whole box with your favorite color.
9. Print a capital and a lower-case **Q** with your black crayon.
10. Draw a picture of a turtle. Print the letter it begins with.
11. Make a red ball. Print the word *stop*.
12. Print your name.

Tell the children, "You have now made a listening quilt. You may color and decorate the edges of this quilt, too."

Quiet-Down Quilts

Let the children design and draw quilts that they imagine would help quacking ducks quiet down. Encourage them to make many capital and lower-case **Q**s on their quilts.

Sound of Q

Teach the children that the sound of **Q** is "kw." Explain that a **Q** is always followed by the letter **U**. Look in a dictionary and show the children the section on **Q**. Make a list of **Q** words for the children to read with you.

MATHEMATICS ACTIVITIES

Quart

Introduce the concept of a quart to the children. Set up a liquid measuring center in which children can experiment filling quart bottles and containers. Provide measuring cups and spoons for them to discover how much of different quantities makes up a quart. Use water as the measuring ingredient.

Quarterback Numbers

Use tagboard to cut out a large quarterback for the bulletin board. Arrange paper footballs all around him within reach of the children. Cut out paper circles with the numbers you have introduced on them, and put them in a box by the bulletin board. Have the children take turns picking a number, naming it, and attaching it to a football. Let the children reverse the game by taking the numbers off the footballs and putting them back into the box. Adapt the game to set recognition, adding, or subtracting.

Quiet Pickup

Discuss how we clean up and recycle trash. Scatter scraps of colored paper over the floor. Give the signal "**Q!**" for everyone to pick up all the scraps they can without making any noise. Have the children count the number of items picked up. Make a chart with the children's names and the number of scraps each picked up.

SCIENCE ACTIVITIES

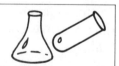

Quiet Animals

Teach the children about some animals that are very quiet and how they use silence to protect themselves. Some quiet animals are rabbits, mice, insects, deer, snakes, lizards, and fish. Make a picture chart of quiet animals, and have the children make one, too. Tell them to use words to label their pictures of animals.

Call It Quits

Conduct this experiment with the children. Place a candle in a jar and light it. Let the children see what happens as you screw a lid on the jar. Help them understand that fire needs air to keep burning.

MOVEMENT AND GAMES

Quarterback Game

Choose two children to be opposing quarterbacks. Clip a capital **Q** to one and a lower-case **q** to the other. Give them one eraser apiece marked with **Q**s to put on their heads. Have them walk around the room in opposite directions; when they meet, have them bow to each other, saying the letter **Q**. If a child loses an eraser, he or she must start over again. The other child waits. If neither loses the eraser, they quickly proceed the rest of the way around the room and pick other quarterbacks to take their places.

Double Circle and a *Q*

Arrange the children into an outer and an inner circle. Tape or chalk a **Q** on the floor inside the inner circle. The outer circle should have one more player than the inner. Have the children skip around in opposite directions. When you call "**Q!**" the children must stop and find a partner from the other circle. The player who is left goes into the center, "a quiet house."

Too Late for the Quarter

Ask the children to join hands in a circle. Choose someone to carry a quarter around the circle and drop it between two children. Those two children run around the circle in opposite directions, trying to get back first and pick up the quarter. Everyone chants to the one who was last, "You're too late for the quarter! You're too late for the quarter!" The child who picked up the quarter continues the game by walking around the circle and dropping it again.

ALPHABET APPETIZER

Quacker Pizzas

Provide a cracker for each child. Have the children top their crackers with ½ teaspoon ketchup or tomato sauce, a slice of cheese to fit the cracker, and a piece of pepperoni or some crumbled, fried hamburger. Put the quacker pizzas in a covered electric skillet, and set on low heat until the cheese is soft and the meat warm.

A QUIET QUIZ

Look at the pictures below. If a picture is of something quiet, write **Q** on the line. If it is of something that makes a noise, write **N** on the line. Practice making **Q**s on the back of this paper.

MY LISTENING QUILT

Listen quietly as your teacher tells you what to do in each box.

1	2	3
4	5	6
7	8	9
10	11	12

Rr

Reindeer

Show the children how to make reindeer by tracing their two hands for antlers and one of their feet for the head. Have the children cut out the shapes and glue the antlers to the head. Have them cut out eyes and a red nose for the reindeer.

Round Rings

Have the children decorate 1-by-6-inch strips of paper with **R**s and other designs. Have them glue or staple the ends of the strips to form rings in a chain. Have the children make their own chains or a very long one as a class to decorate the room for **Rr** week.

Rocking Horses

Give each child a small paper plate. show the children how to fold it in half so that it "rocks." Have them draw and cut out a horse and glue it onto one side of the plate. Add decorations such as rickrack, buttons, and other trims.

Rabbits

Have the children paint pictures of rabbits after you have read them a story about rabbits. Ask each child to tell you something special about the picture for you to write down. Have the children find all the **R**s in their words and make round, red rings around them.

Rings

Have each child imagine and draw a picture of a special magic ring. Encourage each child to tell the others what the ring can do.

Rainbows

Have the children paint rainbows with water colors or tempera paint. Ask them to tell you where they think rainbows come from. Write their responses down and attach them to their pictures.

Reading

Set up a reading center for the children. Place in it a variety of books at different reading levels. Include picture books, alphabet books, and some easy-to-read books. Put in a rocker, some pillows, and soft rugs for the children to relax on as they read.

Red

Teach the children to read the word *red*. Have the children look in magazines and catalogs for pictures of things that are red. Make a large red rooster for a wall or bulletin board in the classroom. Have the children cut out pictures of red things and attach them to the rooster. Encourage them to write the names of the pictures they cut out.

Remember

Play this game with small groups of children. Bring some articles to school that begin with the letter **R**. Show the children the articles and put them away again in the box you brought them in. Then have them try to remember all the things in the box. Some things you might bring are rope, ribbon, rice, rings, rocks, a radio, a rose, a rabbit (toy), raisins, a rectangle, and something round.

Reading Rodeo

Invite some older children into your classroom to read favorite stories to small groups of the children. If possible, hold this "reading rodeo" for several days so the children will have an opportunity to hear many of the older children read. Discuss the stories with the children, and give them a chance to tell which ones they liked best and why.

Relay Race

Divide the class into two equal lines as teams. Name the teams the rabbits and the raccoons. At the signal "**R**!" the right player from each team races to the chalkboard and writes the numeral 1. That player runs back, taps the shoulder of the next child, saying "**R**!"

and sits down at the end of the line. The second child writes a 2, the third a 3, and so on. Continue the game until each child has had a turn. The first team whose players are all sitting down is the winner.

Radio Numbers

Bring a radio to school. Discuss with the children what it is and why people have them. Turn to a station and listen for a while. Have the children listen for numbers. Write the numbers on a chart as they are heard.

Rulers

Introduce the ruler to small groups of children. Prepare a worksheet with lines for the children to measure with rulers. On each line, have them write the numeral representing the length of the line. Let them measure things in the room, such as blocks, boxes, and tables. Lead them to use the language of *longer, shorter, equal,* and *length*.

Rice

Set up a measuring center for the classroom. Put a container of rice in the center of a large tablecloth or blanket. Provide measuring cups, spoons, knives for leveling, and many different containers. Introduce to the children the terms *half, fourth, whole,* and *eighth*. Encourage them to experiment to discover how many of the smaller measures equal larger ones, for example, how many fourths are in 1 cup.

SCIENCE ACTIVITIES

Raisins

Provide for each child a small sheet of aluminum foil with a few grapes on it. Have the children press-write their names on the foil. Let them observe what happens to the grapes from day to day. Encourage the children to keep a record of the changes by drawing pictures of the way they look on different days.

Ranger Rick

Bring in a collection of *Ranger Rick* magazines for the science center, and let the children browse through them. Read the children stories and articles they are interested in. If possible, let the children cut pictures out of the magazines to make little books about animals.

MOVEMENT AND GAMES

Ropes

Use pieces of rope to help improve small-muscle development. Let the children practice tying and untying knots in them.

Robots

Ask the children to move as robots when you give them commands. Begin with easy commands that have two-part directions, such as "Touch your toes and then your nose." Then increase the difficulty of the commands.

Roundup

Choose ten children to be a "roundup" team. Have them join hands in a line. Have the rest of the children be reindeer. When you call "R!" have the roundup team chase the reindeer and attempt to surround one or more of them. To capture the reindeer, have the two children on the ends of the line join hands, forming a circle. As the reindeer are captured, they become part of the roundup team.

Rocking

Have the children lay on their stomachs on the floor. Have them grasp their feet with their hands and make their bodies rock. Show two children how to rock together by sitting and facing each other on the floor with feet extended in front of them. Their feet should be touching. Holding hands with their partners, they rock forward and backward.

ALPHABET APPETIZER

Rockets

Give each child a piece of lettuce, a pineapple ring, half of a banana, and a raisin. Show the children how to assemble a rocket. Have them lay the lettuce on a plate. On top of the lettuce, have them lay the pineapple ring and make the banana stand up inside the pineapple ring. Finally, have them stick the raisin into the top of the banana with a toothpick for a light. **R-R-R-R-R-R-**Blast off!

RHYMING REINDEER

Cut out the circles at the bottom of the page. Find the pairs of words that rhyme and glue one pair onto each reindeer's antlers. On the back of this paper, draw pictures of two things that rhyme.

FIND THE ROCKET

Look at the numbers on each of the sections. Color them according to the key at the bottom of the page. If you color the picture the right way, you will find a rocket. On the back of this paper, draw three rockets aimed toward the right side of the paper.

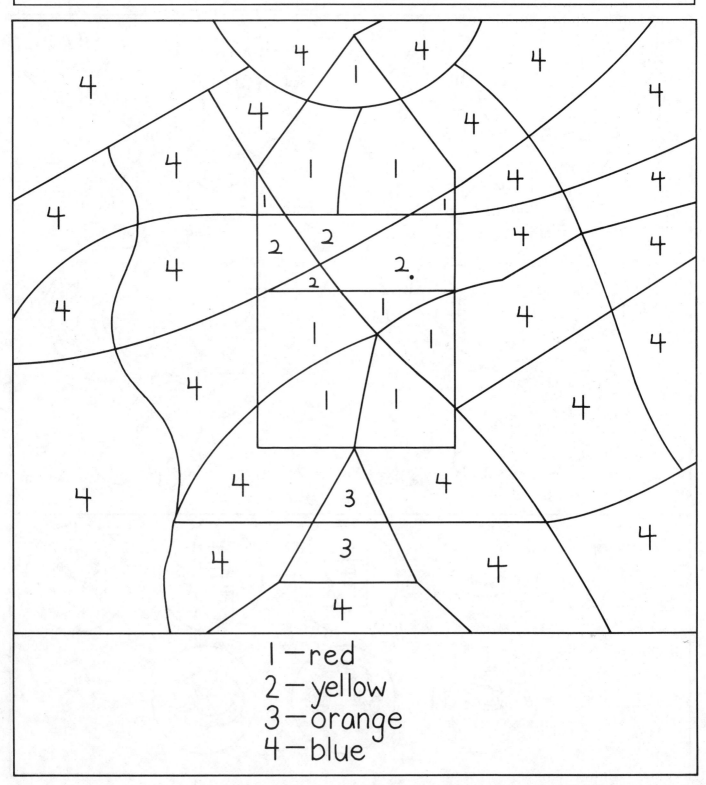

1—red
2—yellow
3—orange
4—blue

Ss

Scribble Art

Have the children scribble with a black crayon on light-colored paper. Then have them use other colors to color in the sections between the scribbled lines, making designs. Ask them to try always to put different colors next to each other.

Spooky Spiders

Give each child an egg-carton section to paint black. Have them use contrasting colors to paint on spots and other decorations. When the paint is dry, have them glue on eight paper legs or attach eight pipe-cleaner legs. Have them think up silly **S** names for their spiders.

Straw Blowing

Let the children experiment with the technique of blowing paint through straws. First, have them spoon different colors of liquid tempera paint onto a sheet of construction paper. Have the children hold straws that have been cut in half and blow the paint around in different directions, creating designs.

Snowstorms

Give each child a baby-food jar. Have the children paper-punch holes out of white typing paper and fill the jars about one-fourth full of holes. Help each child fill the rest of the jar with water and put the lid on tightly. When the children shake the jar—a snowstorm!

Snails

Have each child make a snail by embedding a large macaroni shell into a piece of clay. Have the children set the snails on pieces of heavy cardboard and color the snails' "land" with markers. Show the children how to make eyes and a mouth in the clay section of the snail by poking holes with the point of a pencil.

S Scrapbooks

Have the children cut out pictures of things beginning with the letter **S** and glue them onto pieces of paper. Let the children put the pages together and add a cover for a scrapbook. Show them how to punch holes and tie the pages together with yarn.

Suitcase Game

Bring to school a number of little articles in a small suitcase to use for memory training with small groups of children. Lay the things out for them to see. Talk about each one so that they will know what it is. Then have the children take turns blinding their eyes while you remove something. Have the blindfolded children remove their blinds and tell you what is missing.

Scissors

Let the children use scissors during **Ss** week for special cutting projects. Have them cut **S**s, things that begin with the letter **S**, or **S**-shaped pictures and designs.

Sign Making

Provide a variety of letter patterns for the children to trace for making signs. On a chart, print some typical sign words, such as *stop, go, exit, school,* and *hospital*. Have the children make up some signs of their own names and those of friends.

Supermarket

Have the children pretend they are in a supermarket, and ask them to think of and name all the things beginning with a certain letter that they could buy. Extend this activity by cutting out pictures of items found in a supermarket. Have the children sort them into sacks labeled with beginning sounds.

Scales

Bring a simple scale to the math center. Let the children weigh various objects and record the weights. Have them discuss which objects weigh more and which weigh less.

Six and Seven

Work with the children on the numerals 6 and 7. Teach the children how to form them correctly. Have them practice writing them, construct sets of those amounts, and identify sets with those numbers of things.

Sizes

Find many objects for the children to arrange according to size. Use spoons, measuring cups, pencils, cans, pieces of paper, cut-up straws, lengths of string or yarn, and stacking toys.

SCIENCE ACTIVITIES

Sound

Set a ticking clock on a table. Have the children put their ears against the table and listen for the sound. Explain to them that sound can travel through wood as well as through air.

Spiders

Find a large glass jar to use as a home for a spider. Place a house or garden spider into the jar, along with a small branch and some dirt with grass or a plant. Punch holes in the lid of the jar. Have the children bring in live insects to feed to the spider. With the children, watch the actions of the spider as it spins a web. Let the children use magnifying glasses to observe the spider's movements. Have the children draw pictures of spiders, and help them write down some simple facts that they have learned about spiders.

Seeds

Have the children plant seeds and watch them sprout and grow. Seeds that are fun and easy to grow are beans, corn, sunflowers, squash, and marigolds.

MOVEMENT AND GAMES

Movements for S

Have the children move to music in the play area. Suggest that they sweep, seesaw, crawl like snails, swing, sway, swim, and scamper like squirrels.

Snakes

Have two children hold the ends of a rope and shake it like a snake wriggling on the floor. Tell the other children to form a line and take turns jumping over the rope as it moves, being careful not to touch it.

Sitting Race

Have the children sit side-by-side in a long row with their arms folded and their legs out in front of them. Have them race to a finish line by sitting and moving legs and hips.

Skipping

When teaching children the skill of skipping, try one of these methods: (1) jump and kick on alternate feet; (2) step and hop on alternate feet; or (3) carry a small ball or beanbag and hop along, touching it to each lifted knee.

Snail Shell

Have the children stand in a circle holding hands. Take one child's hand and start walking into the circle, winding in like the spiral of a snail shell. When you reach the center, have the entire line turn and retrace its steps. Direct the children to hold hands firmly at all times, or the snail shell will break.

Stamping

Play some loud music and have the children stamp around like giants. Have them make the sound of **S** and stretch their legs as they stamp around.

ALPHABET APPETIZER

Sprout Salad

Sprout some mung bean or alfalfa seeds the first day of the week. Put them in a quart jar and cover with water overnight. Use 2 tablespoons of seeds for each quart jar. Drain well and secure an old nylon stocking over the top of the jar with a rubber band. Set the jar on its side in a warm place in indirect light. Rinse the seeds twice a day and drain well. The seeds will sprout in about four days. When the sprouts are large enough to eat, have the children cut up lettuce into bite-size pieces and put into small bowls. Top with sprouts. If desired, serve the sprout salad with a dressing.

SEVEN SOCK SIZES

Cut out the seven socks. Arrange them in a line starting with the smallest sock on the left. Glue them down onto a sheet of paper in order, from the smallest to the largest. Trace over the **S**s and color the socks.

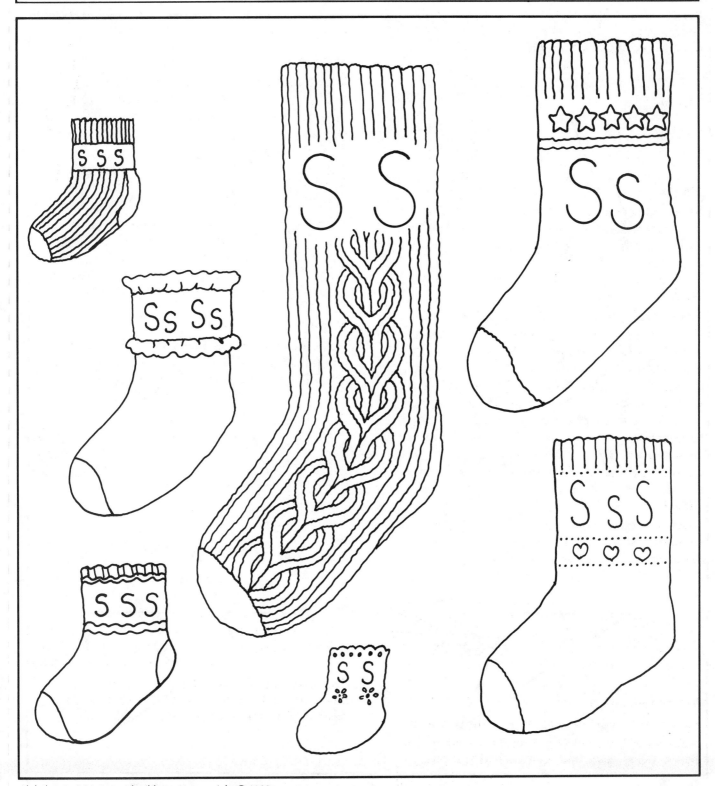

77

STEPS TO THE STARS

Follow the steps below to form a star. Trace over each step, and practice on your own. On the back of this paper, draw a sky full of stars. Make each star smile by putting a happy face in the center.

1.

2.

3.

4.

5.

Tt

Torn-Paper Art

Have the children tear paper shapes to create a picture or design. Have them close their eyes while tearing. Tell them to add features by coloring with crayons or by cutting out things and gluing them on.

Tulips

Show the children how to make tulips by cutting a pocket shape and then cutting tiny triangles from the top of it. Have them cut out several tulips of different colors and glue them down onto a sheet of paper. Have them add stems and leaves.

Tiny Turtles

Have the children form turtles out of play dough or clay. When the dough has dried, let the children paint their turtles. Shellac the turtles to make them shiny.

Topsy-Turvy Time

Ask the children to imagine something that would be topsy-turvy, such as a cat chasing a dog, a giraffe that flies, or a horse in a tree. Have them draw pictures of their topsy-turvy things.

Cup of Tea

Have each child design and cut out a special **T**. Make a large cup for a wall or bulletin board. Put up the children's **T**s above the cup and prepare the caption "Our Cup of **T**."

Tie Turkey

Have the children bring in old ties. Stuff a doubled circle of butcher paper to attach to the bulletin board for the body of a turkey. Cut out and pin on a neck, head, and legs. Arrange the ties around the body for the tail. Have the children write "**T** is for turkey" on paper strips. Pin the strips around the turkey.

READING AND WRITING READINESS

Letter Train

Choose one child to be the engine for a train. Have that child call a letter and start moving slowly around the classroom. Have the other children raise their hands if they know words beginning with that letter. Have the engine call on them, and if they are right, have them join the train by holding onto the waist of the child in front of them. Ask the children on the train to make the sound of the letter as they chug around the room. Choose new engines and letters often, using all the letters you have introduced.

Tracing

Provide cardboard patterns of animal shapes with the names of the animals printed on them. Let the children trace various animals and print their names. Include capital and lower-case **T**s for tracing too.

T Trail

Prepare a trail on paper for each child. Have the children write **T**s and **T** words on the trail to fill it up. Some **T** words that are important for them to learn are *the, to, this, ten, two,* and *too*.

*T*s and Towers

Provide an assortment of building blocks for the children. Have them build tall **T**s and towers.

Tinkertoys

Provide Tinkertoys for the children to build with during **Tt** week. Have them build **T** things, such as turtles, towers, tents, toys, tables, tigers, trains, and tunnels.

MATHEMATICS ACTIVITIES

Time

Bring in real and toy clocks, hourglasses, and old watches for the children to observe. Teach the children to tell time on the hour and half-hour. Introduce the concept of counting by fives as they count on the clock. Discuss how seasons, days of the week, and months are also measurements of time.

Two, Ten, and Twelve

Teach the children to write the numerals 2, 10, and 12, how to make sets of them, and how to identify sets with those numbers of objects. Ask them to write the numbers 1–20 and circle all the numbers beginning with **T**.

Triangles

Teach the children to identify the triangle shape. Ask them to find examples of triangles in the room. Make some triangle patterns for them to trace to make triangle creations. Use games with triangular pieces to help children become familiar with them. Make a triangle-trail game by drawing about 50 triangles for a path. Make a spinner with numerals on it. Show children how to play the game by spinning the spinner and moving that number of spaces along the trail. The first child to reach the end of the triangle trail is the winner.

SCIENCE ACTIVITIES

Turtles

Read some simple books about turtles to the children. Bring one or more turtles into the classroom for observation. Let the children feel the shell of the turtle. Feed the turtle lettuce, bits of beef, and small, live insects. Have the children make turtle charts or booklets to demonstrate what they have learned about turtles.

Tin-Can Telephones

Provide each child with two tin cans that have one end removed and a hold punched in the other end. Have the children put a length of string into the holes and secure the string onto a nail or button. Let the children stretch the string tightly between two of them to talk and listen to each other. Paper cups can be used in place of tin cans.

Tails

Teach the children to look closely at pictures of animals. Ask them to notice each animal's tail. Prepare a bulletin board or folder game of animals without their tails. Put the tails in a separate container for the children to match the correct tail to each animal.

MOVEMENT AND GAMES

Tying

Provide old shoes, ropes, string, and laces for the children to practice tying. Let the children help each other learn to tie. After they have had time to practice, ask them to draw and cut out a large triangle with a happy face. Staple two lengths of yarn to the triangle and have the children tie them.

Tumbling

Introduce the children to tumbling on mats. Begin with simple stunts such as log rolls, forward somersaults, the crab walk, and the arm walk with legs dragging behind.

Tires

Lay old tires around the gym or play area. Have the children use them to run around, skip around, walk around the rims, walk and run through, step in and out of, stand and jump inside, and crawl through while someone holds the tire upright. The children also can roll them around, set them up and toss balls and beanbags through them, stand in the centers and jump out of them, jump from one to another as they are lying close together, frog-jump in and out of them, walk around them on hands and feet frontwards and backwards, and have relays with them.

Tortoise and Hare

Have the children stand in a group facing you. When you call ''Tortoise!'' have them walk very slowly in place. When you call ''Hare!'' have them run in place with quick steps. When you call ''T!'' have them stand still, making their body in the shape of a lower-case **T**.

ALPHABET APPETIZER

Tasty Toast

Have each child toast a slice of whole wheat bread and spread it with butter. Ask them to choose other toppings if desired, such as peanut butter, honey, or cinnamon sugar. Have them cut the toast into triangles.

TURKEY TALK

Many words end with the sound of **T**. Cut out the tail feathers on the bottom of the page and glue them onto the turkey, next to the words they represent. On the back of this paper, draw a turkey. Make **T**s on each of its tail feathers.

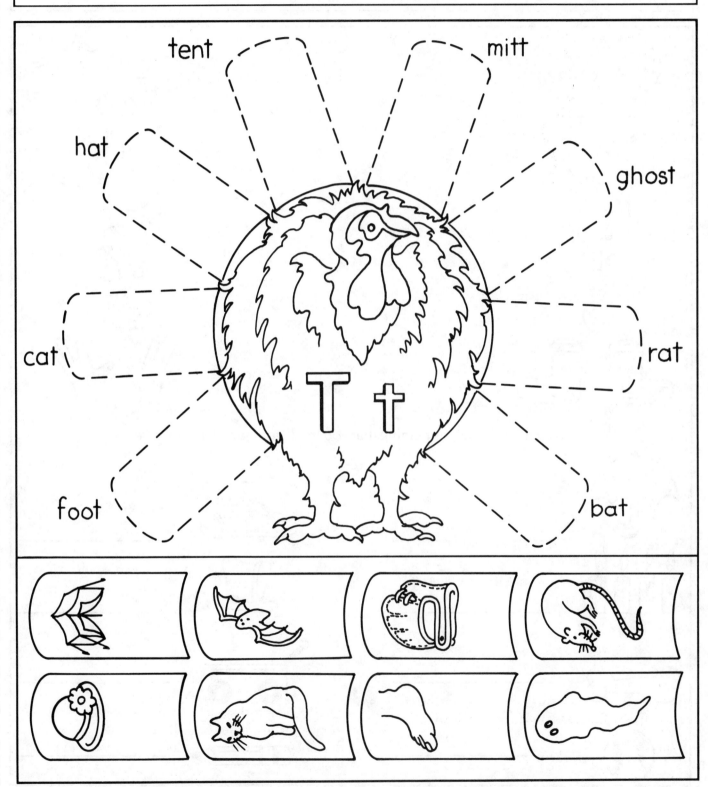

tent

mitt

hat

ghost

cat

rat

foot

bat

T t

TOGETHER TIME

Draw a line from the picture on the left to the thing on the right that it goes with. On the back of this paper, practice printing **T**s.

On each line, draw something that you think goes with each picture.

ART ACTIVITIES

UgUgUg Creatures

Have the children use their imaginations to make space creatures from the planet UgUgUg. Provide a variety of materials such as paper, glue, sewing trims, pipe cleaners, Q-tips, buttons, string, and yarn.

Unicorns

Show the children pictures of unicorns in books or on posters. Ask them to paint unicorns. Have them tell stories about their unicorns for you to write down on their paintings. Have them find and underline the **U**s in their words.

Umbrellas

Have the children cut individual egg-carton cups in half. Show them how to glue the halves onto sheets of construction paper. Have them add pipe-cleaner handles to make umbrellas. Have them make pictures around the umbrellas with their crayons. If they like, the children can decorate the umbrellas with paint or markers.

Find the *U*

Have the children color heavily on a sheet of paper, using several different crayons. Then have them use a popsicle stick to etch out a capital and a lower-case **U** and an umbrella.

Up, Up, Up!

Have the children make hot-air balloons that go up. First have them cut out a balloon and paint it with bright colors. Next have them connect the balloon to a basket they have cut out by gluing paper strips to the basket and to the balloon. Ask them to decorate the balloons with the word *up* and the letter **U**. Display the balloons with the caption "**U** Is for Up!"

READING AND WRITING READINESS

Unicorn Books

Prepare empty books for the children to illustrate stories about unicorns. Write out their words for them as they tell you the story. Ask them to find and underline the **U**s in their stories. Invite another class into your room and let the children share their stories.

Imaginary Uncles

Divide the children into small groups. Tell them to make up stories and pictures of an uncle they would like to have—for example, an uncle with magic powers. When they have illustrated the pictures, tape them all together and roll them onto tubes attached to a box for an "Uncle Movie." Let the children tell about their imaginary uncles as you turn the pictures.

Uncle Stories

As a take-home project, ask the children and their parents to talk about a special uncle of theirs. Provide time for the children to tell about their uncles and show pictures they have drawn of them.

Sound of *U*

Teach the children the short sound of **U** by comparing it to the sound that someone might make if punched in the stomach. Have them practice making the sound and listening for it in words. Tell them that **U** has a long sound, too, such as in the words *unicorn* and *ukelele*.

MATHEMATICS ACTIVITIES

Umbrellas in the Rain

Prepare a game for the children to play in small groups. Make umbrellas from colored construction paper for the numbers you have introduced, writing a number on each one. Cut out several raindrops for each number with the set connotation on each. Have the children match the correct raindrops to umbrellas.

U Puzzles

Cut out the letter **U** for each number you want the children to practice. Write the numeral on the **U** and a set of dots representing that numeral. Make the **U**s into puzzles by cutting them apart between the section with the numeral and the dots. Put them into a colorful container for the children to solve.

SCIENCE ACTIVITIES

Underground

Take the children outdoors to dig in an area of dirt. Let them discover the kinds of animals that are found underground. Show them books and filmstrips depicting life underground. Divide the class into groups to make murals of what is underground.

Underwater

Provide an assortment of shells for the children to look at and touch. Tell them that shells are found underwater at the bottom of seas and oceans. Teach them the names of various shells. Provide books, pictures, and filmstrips about shells and other underwater items.

Up

Have the children make posters with pictures of all the things they can think of that go up. Have them label the pictures using a chart you have prepared to help them. Examples of things that go up are airplanes, helicopters, hot-air balloons, balloons, gliders, kites, birds, butterflies, flying insects, rockets, and spaceships.

MOVEMENT AND GAMES

Swing Around the *U*

Divide the children into two teams, and pair the children up on each team. On the signal "U!" the first pair from each team joins hands and runs to **U**s that you have taped to the floor. They must swing around in a circle with joined hands. Have them return to their team and tap the next pair of racers, saying "**U**" as they do so. The first team to finish wins.

Under Cover

Work with the concept of "under" by bringing several old sheets to the gym. Divide the children into groups so that there will be four or five children around each sheet. Have them hold on to the sheet and perform the actions you call out. When you call "Under!" have them all get under the sheet and pull it around themselves. Some actions to call are: run in a circle to the right and the left; walk in a circle to the right and the left; skip in a circle to the right and the left; crawl in a circle to the right and the left; pull the sheet tight, shake the sheet, and put a beanbag or a ball on the sheet and make it bounce; and lift the sheet up quickly and let it go.

Umbrella Game

Have the children line up and then have the line form a circle with children standing behind each other. Play some music as you direct the children to march through an "umbrella" formed by two children holding their arms up high. When the music stops, have them put their arms down, at which point the person under the umbrella goes to the center of the circle. When a second person is trapped under the umbrella, he or she forms a new umbrella with the child in the center of the circle. Continue the game until five umbrellas have been formed.

Under the Rope

Have the children experiment with all the ways they can think of to move under a rope. Have them take turns holding the ends of the rope as the others go under. Play this game in the same way as "Follow the Leader" so that all the children can try moving in different ways.

ALPHABET APPETIZER

Under My Umbrella

Let each child measure ¼ cup of cottage cheese and put it on a small paper plate. Provide a variety of fruits for the children to cut up, such as pears, apples, a pineapple, bananas, peaches, and oranges. Have the children arrange the cut-up fruits on the cottage cheese in the shape of the letter **U**. Let each child wash and dry a piece of lettuce for an umbrella to cover the **U** until it is time to eat.

UGLIES EVERYWHERE!

Count the Uglies on each umbrella. Write the number for each under the umbrellas. On the back of this paper, draw a big umbrella and write capital and lower-case **U**s all over it.

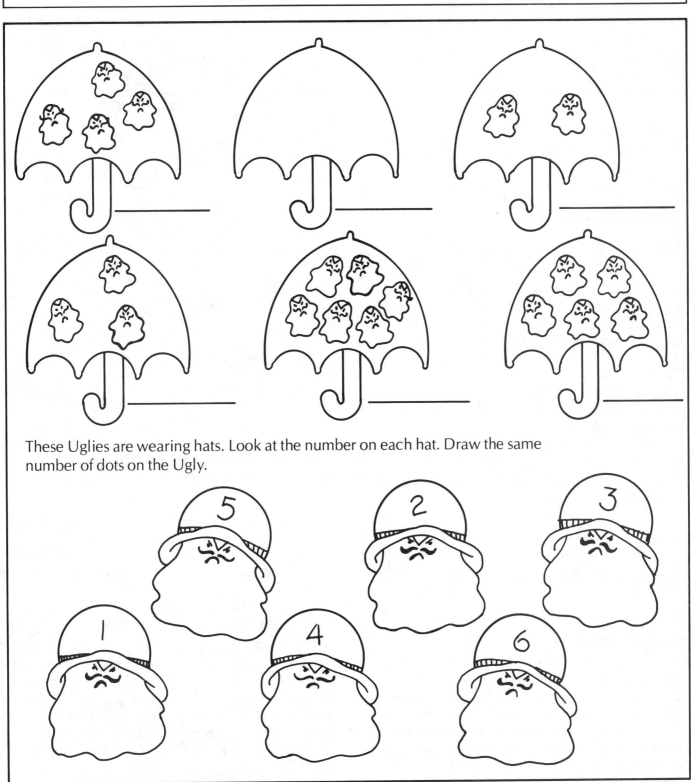

These Uglies are wearing hats. Look at the number on each hat. Draw the same number of dots on the Ugly.

U
SURPRISES

Do this dot-to-dot picture. Find the letter **A** first, then follow the rest of the alphabet.

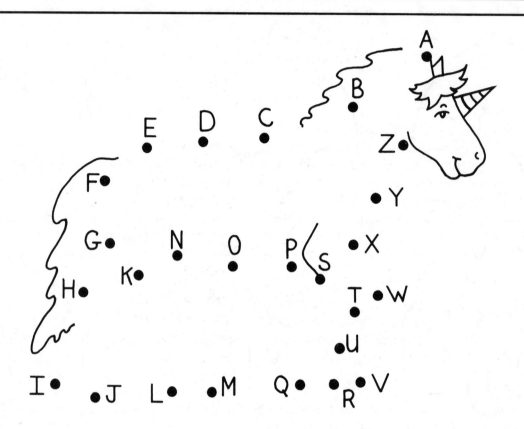

Here are two more dot-to-dot pictures. Connect the lower-case letters in order for these. On the back of this paper, make a dot-to-dot picture of your own.

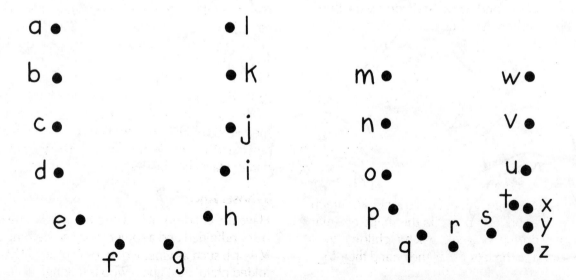

Alphabet Activities reproducible page, copyright © 1983

Vampire Mix-Up

Play this game with small groups of children. Make a set of vampires so that you have one for each of the basic colors. Lay the vampires out in a certain order. Have the children take turns blinding their eyes while you or another child rearranges the order of the vampires. The child whose blindfold has been removed must try to put the vampires back in their original order. Make this game more difficult by adding some colored **V**s to the group of vampires.

Vampire Story

Write a language-experience story with the children about a make-believe vampire. Have them sit around you so they can watch you form letters and write words. Ask them to help you spell words and think of the ideas for the story. Look for **V**s in the story. Read it together with the class when it is finished. Have the children illustrate the story. Display the story and pictures for other children in the school to see and read.

V-Word Puzzles

On strips of tagboard, write **V** words with the letters spaced apart. Make puzzle by cutting between the letters. Put the puzzle pieces into envelopes with the **V** words printed on the outside. Provide materials for the children to make some puzzles of their own.

Verses

Explain the term *verse* to the children. Read nursery rhymes and sing some simple songs that have verses. Ask the children to help create a new song with new verses for "Old Vam Vampire Had a Valley," using "Old MacDonald Had a Farm" as the model.

Voices

Tell the children to recite a favorite poem or sing a favorite song. Tape-record it. Let the children listen to their voices. Tape one child at a time saying a sentence about some **V** thing and then saying his or her name. Have the class listen to the voices.

Whose Voice?

Have the children sit in a circle. Choose one child to be blindfolded and another to say something about a **V** word, such as *vine, violet,* or *vampire.* The blindfolded child must guess who is talking.

ART ACTIVITIES

Vampires

Provide different shades of violet paper for the children to make vampires by cutting and gluing body parts together and adding features. Give each child a piece of nylon netting for a veil over their vampire's face. Have them staple or glue on the netting. Ask the children to give their vampires **V** teeth and a **V**-shaped nose. Have the children tell something about their vampires while showing them during circle time.

Vegetable Prints

Have the children cut up a variety of vegetables to use for printing. Provide different colors of paint for different vegetables. Use potatoes, cabbage, onions, green peppers, celery, carrots, and zucchini.

Valentine Hangings

Have the children cut out three white hearts (see the Hearts activity on p. 31). Provide a pattern for them to trace, if desired. Have them glue the hearts onto a strip of red construction paper 12 inches long and 2 inches wide. Have the children write *I* on the first heart, *love* on the second heart, and *you* on the third heart. Let the children decorate the hangings.

Variety of *V*s

Have each child design and cut out a fancy **V**. Attach these to a wall or bulletin board in the shape of a giant **V** for a display during **Vv** week. Ask the children to make the sound of the letter **V** as they hand their **V**s to you.

Sound of *V*

Teach the children to make the sound of the letter **V** by placing their top teeth over their bottom lip and buzzing. Tell them it is like the sound of a vacuum cleaner. Have them practice making the sound and listening for words with the sound.

MATHEMATICS ACTIVITIES

Vampire Blindfold

Blindfold a child to be the vampire. Give the vampire a pointer with a **V** taped to it. Have the children march in a circle around the vampire until the vampire says "**V**!" and points with the pointer. Whichever child the vampire is pointing to then begins to count. The vampire must guess who is counting. Adapt this game for reciting the alphabet.

Vision Work

Provide patterns of different shapes and numbers for the children to copy. Make the patterns in varying degrees of difficulty. Have the children copy the patterns, doing as many different patterns as possible.

Valentine Sorting

Provide a box of old valentines for the children to use for sorting. Let them sort according to size, pictures, hearts, or any other categories the children think of. Have them count the number of words on each valentine and sort them that way.

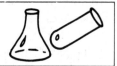

SCIENCE ACTIVITIES

Vegetables

Provide a variety of food pictures, including some from each food group. Have the children sort them according to "vegetables" and "not vegetables." Bring in some uncommon vegetables to teach the children about, and cut them up for a tasting experience. Help the children learn to identify several new vegetables.

Vase Gardens

Suspend a sweet potato, potato, onion, or avocado in a glass jar with toothpicks. Let the children watch the roots grow.

Vehicles

Teach the children the term *vehicle*. Have the children make charts or books of all the vehicles they can think of. Provide dictionaries for them to use to help write words for each of their pictures.

MOVEMENT AND GAMES

Vibrating Volcanos

Let the children use their imaginations and pretend their bodies are vibrating volcanos. Have them make the sound of **V** as they vibrate.

Volleyball

Divide the children into two teams, and ask them to spread out on each side of a low net or a row of chairs. Have them throw a ball back and forth, trying not to let it touch the floor. Use tally marks to keep score for the teams on a chalkboard or chart.

Vans

Ask the children to pretend to be vans in the gym or on a play area. Have them make the sound of **V** as they drive around. When you call "Red light!" the vans must stop. Have the children listen carefully as you tell them to drive, stop, back up, go sideways, drive slowly, drive fast, drive in pairs, go around corners, go up hills, and come down hills.

ALPHABET APPETIZER

Vegetable Village

Divide the children into groups of four or five. Have the children cut vegetables into sticks. Provide carrots, celery, zucchini, peppers, and cucumbers. Provide some cooked peas, beans, and corn for adding features. Give each group a tray to build a little village on. Provide a cheese sauce or a dip for the vegetables.

HOW VIOLETS GROW

Cut out the four pictures of a growing violet at the bottom of this page. Glue them in the right order at the top of the page by matching them with the correct number. On the back of this paper, draw a four-part story about a vampire. Tell the story to someone.

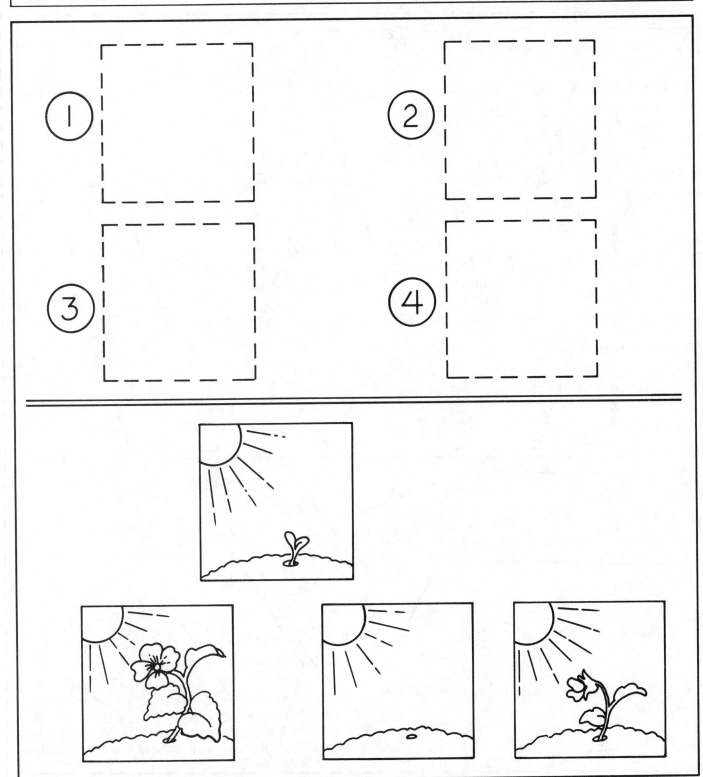

V
PUZZLES

Cut out the pieces of the capital and lower-case **V**s on the bottom of the page. Fit them where they belong on the pattern and glue them down. On the back of this paper, design a vest you would like to have. Be sure to put **V**s on it somewhere.

Alphabet Activities reproducible page, copyright © 1983

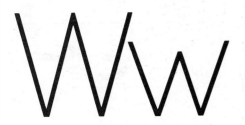

Whales

Have the children paint large whales at the art center. Provide large sheets of paper, black paint for whales, and blue or green paint for water. Ask the children to tell you something special about their whales, and write it down. Have the children find and circle all the **W**s in their words.

Water Paint

Take the children outdoors on a sunny day. Let them work in pairs, using containers of water and paintbrushes to paint pictures on the sidewalks or playground. Ask them to paint some **W**s. If the weather does not permit this, let the children "paint" with water on the chalkboards.

Wind Wheels

Show the children how to make pinwheels by taking a 6-inch square of paper and cutting from the corners to within an inch from the center. Have the children fold every other point to the center, which then is pinned to an eraser at the end of a pencil. Leave it loose enough for the pinwheel to turn.

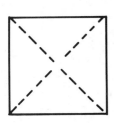

Wallpaper Pictures

Have the children cut out pictures and designs from wallpaper. Have them glue their designs to construction paper and add other features.

Walnut-Shell Boats

Give the children halved walnut shells with which to make boats. Have them stick a small ball of clay into the bottom of the shell to hold a toothpick with a flag they design. Have the children put **W**s on their flags. Let them try to float their boats.

Wax Pictures

Have the children draw a picture or design on colored construction paper with paraffin wax. Then have them paint over the picture with a wash.

Whiskers

Let the children draw and cut out a favorite animal that has whiskers. Have them cut and glue on skinny whiskers of a contrasting color. Show the children how to curl the whiskers around a pencil.

Wood Creations

Provide for the children a box of scrap wood that has been cut into small pieces. Have them glue pieces together to create something. Ask them to name their creations and tell about them at circle time.

Wheel of *W*s

Have the children design and cut out wonderful **W**s. Arrange these on your door or wall in the shape of a wheel. Caption it "Wonderful Wheel of **W**s!"

Witchy ABCs

Ask the children to pretend to be witches and recite their ABCs with their spookiest voices. Have them count this way, too.

Working with Words

Make a list of words for the children to look for in a simple dictionary. Provide them with an empty book or blank paper to illustrate the words as they find them. Include several **W** words in this exercise.

Sound of *W*

Teach the children to make the sound of **W** by forming the lips in a small circle. Have them watch you and then try themselves. Give them opportunities to make and listen for the sound.

MATHEMATICS ACTIVITIES

Weights

Weigh each child and record the weights for the children to read and compare.

Wagon

Bring a wagon to school in which special number games can be put. Have the children stack building blocks in the wagon and count how many they can fit in.

Wigwams

Have the children draw ten wigwams on a sheet of paper. In each wigwam, have them write one of the numerals 1–10 and a corresponding set of **W**s.

SCIENCE ACTIVITIES

What Needs Water?

Have the children cut out pictures for a chart depicting things that need water and things that do not need water.

Wheels

Talk with the children about wheels and how they help us. Have the children find examples of wheels in the classroom. Display pictures of things that have wheels. Show the children how to make a set of wheels by putting a straw through two spools.

Worms

Dig up some worms and bring them to school in a large glass jar filled with dirt. Let the children watch the worms through the glass. Lay a worm out on some paper with soil, and let the children look closely at the worm through magnifying glasses.

Wigwams

Give each child a cup of soil and some toothpicks. Show them how to form a wigwam out of toothpicks in the soil. Have the children plant bean seeds in the center of the wigwam and watch the plants grow up the wigwam.

MOVEMENT AND GAMES

Worms

Have the children pretend to be wiggly, wriggly worms crawling around on the floor. Ask them to greet each other by making the sound of **W**.

Ways of Walking

Experiment with different ways of walking with the children, such as fast, slow, backwards, sideways, heels together, toes together, on heels, on tiptoes, while flapping arms, and with crossover steps. Have the children improvise ways to walk with a wiggle. As they walk around, have them wave to each other.

Whistle Ball

Have the children sit in a circle as a ball is passed around. Whoever is holding the ball when you blow a whistle is out of the circle.

Windmills

Have the children pair up and stand back-to-back, stretching their arms out at their sides. Have them bend down and touch the right leg with the right hand and then the left leg with the left hand. Moving together, each pair makes a windmill.

ALPHABET APPETIZER

Wheaty Wonders

    1 cup unbleached white flour
    1 cup whole wheat flour
    4 teaspoons baking powder
    1 teaspoon salt
    ⅓ cup oil
    ¾ cup milk

Have the children help measure and mix the ingredients. Divide the dough into about 20 parts and have the children knead the dough for a minute. Have them press the dough down so that it is about ¼ inch high. Butter an electric skillet and heat to 350°. Place the dough patties into the electric skillet and fry on each side about 4 minutes until brown. Serve with butter and honey or jam.

WINDOW WATCH

Cut out the "windows" on the bottom of the page. Match the beginning sound in each window with a picture. Glue each window strip with capital **W**s onto a picture strip with lower-case **W**s. Then open your windows.

WORD
WHEEL

Cut out the two wheels below. Put the smaller one on top of the larger one, matching the middle dots. Insert a brass fastener into the dots. Turn the wheels and read the words you can make.

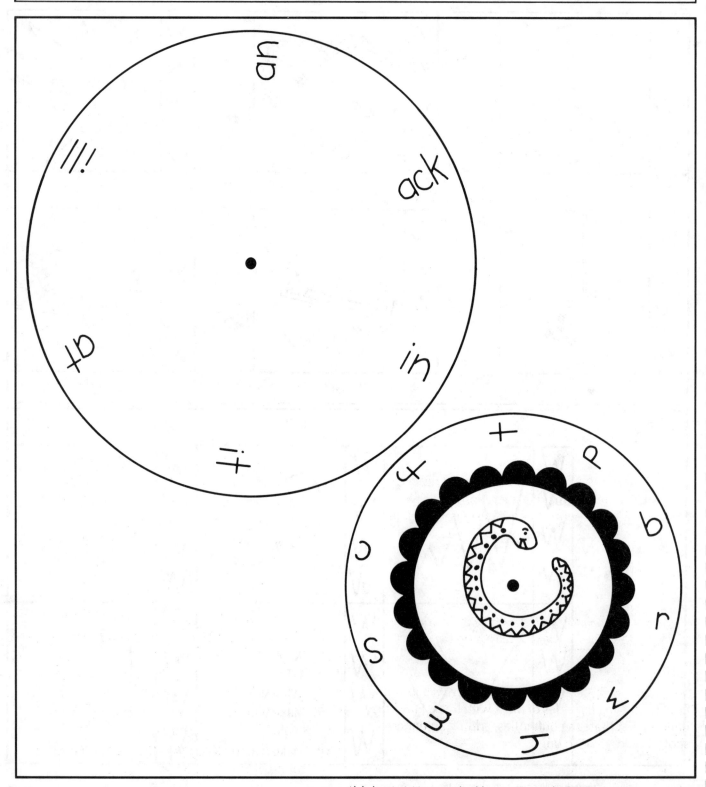

Xx

ART
ACTIVITIES

X-traordinary Puppets

Have each child stuff a paper bag and tie it with yarn or string at the bottom. Have the children use paper to cut out and glue on eyes, ears, an **X** nose, and a mouth. Let them glue on scraps of yarn or draw **X**s all around the top and sides of the sack for hair. Ask them to make **X**s all around the bottom of the sack.

X-Specially Nice Xs

Give the children large sheets of paper on which to draw and decorate **X**s. Ask them to cut them out. Form them into a large **X** for a wall or bulletin board display during **Xx** week.

X Borders

Have the children draw a picture of something having to do with a topic you are studying in the classroom. Ask them to leave a space all around the edge of the picture, and have them make a border of colorful **X**s.

Painted Xs

Give the children a variety of colors of paint. Have them paint a picture making everything out of **X**s—**X** trees, **X** houses, **X** people, and **X** designs. Have the children share their pictures at circle time.

A Garden of Xs

Have the children use their green crayons to make stems for a garden of flowers. Then have them use a variety of colors to design flowers from **X**s for their gardens. Ask them to make **X** leaves on the stems.

Butterfly from an X

Show the children how to make butterfly wings from an **X** by closing the sides of the **X** with lines. Have the children decorate the butterflies, adding antennae, spots, bodies, and so on.

READING AND
WRITING READINESS

X Formations

Give the children different materials with which to form the letter **X**, such as bottle caps, buttons, rocks, and beans.

Building Xs

Provide blocks and Tinkertoys for the children to build large letter **X**s. Have them share their work with the other children before taking it apart.

Sound of X

Teach the children the sound of the letter **X** as the sounds of **K** and **S** blended. Gather the children around you and have them help you spell some simple words ending in **X**. Explain that **X** usually comes at the end of words. (When it comes at the beginning of a word, it makes a different sound.) Examples of words that end in **X** are *fox, sax, Max, ox, ax, fix, mix, six,* and *box.*

A Listening Experience for X

Use the worksheet on page 97 for this lesson. Tape-record the instructions below or read them to the children.

1. With your red crayon, make an **X** on the largest animal on the paper.
2. With your blue crayon, make an **X** on the smallest animal you can see.
3. With your orange crayon, make an **X** on an animal that people ride.
4. With your yellow crayon, make an **X** on an animal that has designs on its wings.
5. With your green crayon, make an **X** on an animal that might be found in trees and that is considered to be wise.
6. With your brown crayon, make an **X** on the animal that swings from tree to tree in the jungle.
7. With your black crayon, make an **X** on the animal that is a pet.
8. With your purple crayon, make an **X** on the animal that swims in the ocean.
9. Make two green **X**s on an animal with a long beak.
10. Make two red **X**s on the animal that makes the sound of **S**.

95

MATHEMATICS ACTIVITIES

Xs to Count

Draw **X**s on about 60 small circles. Have the children form sets for each of the numerals 1–10. Have the children count the circles into paper cups with the numerals written on them.

X Party

Assign numbers to the children in the class, making two of each, such as two 1s, two 2s, and so on. Give the children large cards with their numbers on them to hold in front of them. Seat the children on chairs in a circle. Choose one child to be a caller, who stands in the center of the circle and calls a number. The two children who have that number try to exchange places before the caller takes one of the chairs. If the caller does get a chair, the child standing becomes the new caller.

SCIENCE ACTIVITIES

Water Xylophone

Fill eight glasses with gradually increasing depths of water. "Play" the glasses for the children so they can hear the difference in the sounds made. Let the children repeat the experiment alone or in small groups.

X Nature Collages

Take the children for a walk outdoors. Have them collect sticks, rocks, leaves, and other articles of nature. When back in the classroom, give the children sheets of cardboard or other heavy paper with large **X**s drawn on them. Have the children glue down their found objects onto the **X**.

MOVEMENT AND GAMES

X-Ray X's Orders

Choose a child to be a creature from outer space named **X-Ray X**, and whisper a message in that child's ear. Have the child whisper the message to another child, who must act out the message. Have the other children try to guess what **X-Ray X**'s orders were. Some examples of orders are: *turn around, touch the floor, write on the chalkboard, pretend to sing, roll on the floor,* and *clap hands*.

Musical X

Hide a small ball with **X**s taped to it somewhere in the room while someone is blindfolded. Remove the blindfold and have that child look for the ball. Direct the rest of the children to clap loudly when the person looking is close to the ball and softly as the person gets farther away from it.

Follow the Leader with an X

Ask the children to play "Follow the Leader," performing an **X** motion of some kind while moving. Some ideas are to make an **X** with fingers, hands, arms, and the whole body while running, walking, skipping, hopping, tiptoeing, jumping, or crawling.

X Race

Divide the children into three or more teams of equal sizes. Have the first player on each team race to an **X** taped to the floor at a distance from the beginning spot. When they reach the **X**, have them stop and jump to form an **X** with their bodies. Then have them run back; tap the next person on the shoulder, saying "**X**"; and sit down at the end of their line. The first team with everyone sitting down is the winner.

X People

Have the children pretend to be **X** people. Tell them you will ask them to move in certain ways, at the same time keeping their bodies in an **X** shape. Call out movements such as running, walking, jumping, hopping, leaping, lying down, tiptoeing, and going backward.

ALPHABET APPETIZER

X on an X

Give each child a nutritious cracker or slice of Melba toast. Have the children slice cheese into strips, then cross two strips on their crackers in the shape of the letter **X**. Then have them press raisins or other dried fruit into the cheese, forming another **X**.

MARK **X**

Listen as your teacher tells you to mark these animals with **X**s of different colors. When you are finished, practice making colorful **X**s on the back of this paper.

horse

dog

owl

monkey

butterfly

duck

snail

elephant

fish

snake

97

X THE BOXES

Look at the two things on each box. If they begin with the same sound, make an **X** in the box. If they do not begin with the same sound, print *No* in the box. On the back of this paper, make a box of your own. Put two things in it that begin with the same letter as the first letter of your name.

Alphabet Activities reproducible page, copyright © 1983

ART ACTIVITIES

Yards

Give the children large sheets of white paper to make maps of their yards at home. Provide time for each of them to tell about their yard map.

Yellow Fellows

Provide the children with various shades of yellow paint to paint "yellow fellows." Have them tell something special about their fellow for you to write down. Ask them to find and color the **Y**s in their words.

Yellow Yaks

Have each child make a yellow yak. Show the children how to cut out a yak's body, neck, head, and legs from yellow paper and glue them together. Have them glue on white paper for horns and pieces of yellow yarn for a tail and mane.

Yarn Trees

Collect interesting branches from trees and bushes. If possible, let the children help with this by going on a walk together or asking them to bring some from home. Embed each branch into a ball of clay so that it stands up. Have the children wind yarn pieces of different colors in and out between the sections of the branch, making a spider-web design.

"You" Bulletin Board

Prepare a bulletin board for the classroom with a mirror in the center. Around the mirror, cut out and put up letters that say "You Are Most Important!" Have the children make pictures of parents, grandparents, brothers, and sisters on small circles of paper. Put up the caption "People Who Have Helped Make You What You Are" for the display.

Yarn

Give each child a string of yarn. Have the children identify it and imagine all the things it could be used

for. Have them experiment laying it out in **Y**s, shapes, and designs. Let them tie it, wind it into a ball, make bows with it, and cut it.

Yarn Mobile

Give each child a coat hanger that has been stretched to form a diamond shape. Have the children wrap yarn around the entire hanger, covering the metal. Show them how to cross yarn over from side to side across the diamond, making a design. Tell the children to be sure to wrap the yarn around the hanger each time they get to a side to help hold it in place. Provide a variety of yarn colors for these mobiles.

READING AND WRITING READINESS

Y Words

Teach the children to read the words *you, your, yes,* and *yellow.* Make small flashcards with which the children can practice.

Listening for Y Words

Teach the children the sound of the letter **Y**. Have them practice making the sound. Play a game in which the children make the sound of **Y** when you hold up a letter card with a **Y**. Hold up cards with similar-looking letters, such as **V, v, G, g, J, j, K, k,** and **X**. After this part of the game, say a series of words. When the children hear a word beginning with the sound of **Y**, have them call, "Yea!"

Yellow Things

Gather the children around you while you print on a large chart words for things that are yellow. Let the children do the thinking. Look for **Y**s on the chart and have children take turns circling them with a yellow marker. Have the children draw or cut out pictures of things that are yellow.

MATHEMATICS ACTIVITIES

Yardsticks

Work with small groups of children inspecting yardsticks. Let them measure things in the classroom, count to the numbers on the stick, and compare yard-sticks with other measuring devices.

Yellow Play Dough

Prepare a large batch of yellow play dough. Have the children practice forming numbers and shapes.

Yellow Yolks

Draw and cut out some eggs with yellow yolks. Inside each yolk write an addition problem. Have the children try to solve the problems. On the back of the egg, write the solution so the children can check their answers.

SCIENCE ACTIVITIES

Young

Talk with the children about the differences between grown animals and their young. Show the children books and filmstrips involving baby animals. Have each of them make a book or chart with three of their favorite animals drawn as both young and grown up. Help them label the pictures.

*Y*s in the World

Take the children for a walk outdoors. Ask them to look for the shape of **Y**s in the outside world—the ways branches come together, cracks in sidewalks, shape of trees with branches, and so on. When you return to the classroom, talk with the children about your experience. Have the children draw some of the things they saw on the walk.

Yeast

Teach the children what yeast is. Let them see it and smell it. Ask them if they have ever used it before. Plan a special cooking project in which the children use yeast to make bread. The following recipe takes less than two hours from start to finish.

Let the children help mix and measure 1½ cups warm water, 1½ tablespoons yeast, ¼ cup honey, and 1½ tablespoons oil. Add 3½ cups whole wheat flour, 1 teaspoon salt, and ½ cup powdered milk. Cover the bowl and let the dough rest for about 15 minutes. Divide it into enough balls for each of the children to have one, or take turns with the class kneading the dough for 10 minutes. Have flour ready for the children to use while kneading. Form the dough into the shape of a **Y** and let it rise for 15 minutes in a warm

place. Bake at 375° for about 25 minutes. Slice and serve with butter and honey or jam.

MOVEMENT AND GAMES

Yo-yo Antics

Suspend a yo-yo from the ceiling of the room. Have the children use it for working with eye movements. Ask them to tap it and watch it go from side to side. Let them try to hit it with a plastic bat or bowling pin.

Yellow Yarn Mail

Make a yellow yarn ball for this game. Have the children sit in a circle facing inward. Let them take turns rolling or throwing the yellow yarn, saying, "I'm sending yellow yarn for **Y** to _____ ."

Movements as *Y* Things

Have the children spread out on the play area so they each have room to move about without touching one another. Ask them to pretend to be yogurt in a dish, yaks in a yard, yo-yos being pulled up and down, and people yanking things.

Yakety-Yak in the Yak Yard

Have the children form a circle holding hands. Choose one child to be a "yak" and stand in the center of the circle. Have the yak try to break out between two children. If the yak gets out of the circle, the two children broken through try to catch the yak. If one of them is successful, he or she becomes the new yak.

ALPHABET APPETIZER

Yummy Yogosicles

Have each child measure the following ingredients into a small bowl: ¼ cup yogurt (plain, vanilla, or banana); 1 teaspoon frozen orange juice concentrate, thawed; and 1 teaspoon honey. Tell them to mix well and pour the mixture into a 3-ounce paper or plastic cup, then freeze it. When the mixture is solid enough to hold up a popsicle stick, put one in, then refreeze until firm.

ADD AND COLOR
Ys

Solve the adding problems on the **Y**s. Look at the code at the bottom of the page to see what color to make each section. Trace around the outside of the **Y**s with your black crayon. On the back of this paper, make up five adding problems of your own.

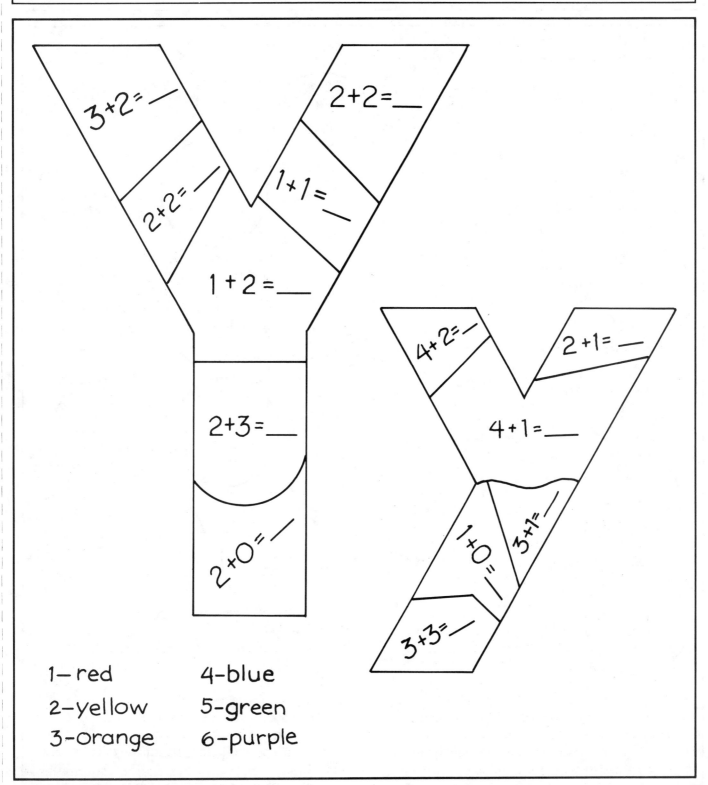

3+2=___
2+2=___
2+2=___
1+1=___
1+2=___
2+3=___
2+0=___

4+2=___
2+1=___
4+1=___
1+0=___
3+1=___
3+3=___

1—red   4—blue
2—yellow   5—green
3—orange   6—purple

WHERE IS THE YAK YARD?

Help the yak get to the yak yard. Color a path of numbered circles in order from 1 to 15. Use your favorite color. On the back of this paper, draw a yak yard and fill it with **Y**s.

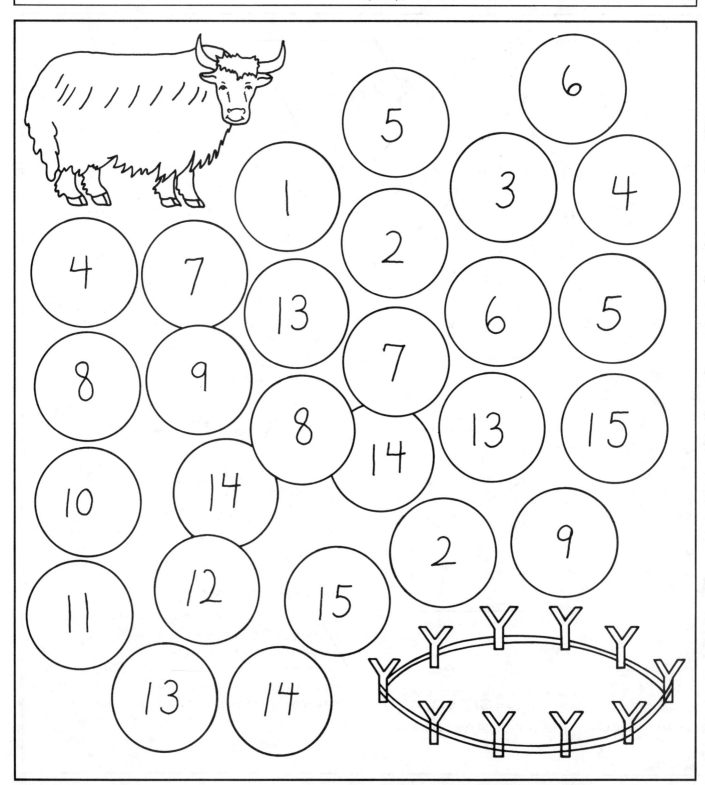

Alphabet Activities reproducible page, copyright © 1983

Zz

Show how to cut the corners off a square to make a circle. Ask the children to cut a circle from each size of paper and attach them in their centers with a brass fastener. Have them push the brass fastener through a sheet of construction paper as a back and open the fastener in the back to secure the flower. Let them add stem and leaves and a bumblebee saying "ZZZZZZ!"

ART ACTIVITIES

Zippy's Zipper

Ask the children to pretend that they have found a magic zipper. Have each child make up an adventure concerning the zipper and tell you about it. Write it down and have the child read it with you. Ask the children to look for and circle all the **Z**s in their words.

Zoo Cages

Ask the children to make their favorite zoo animal by drawing, cutting, and gluing or by painting. Have them make bars for the zoo cage by gluing black paper strips around the edges and over the top of their representations. Have each child make a sign naming the animal in the cage.

Zebras

Have the children paint large pictures of zebras in the zoo. When the pictures have dried, let the children cut the zebras out. Arrange the zebras in the shape of a giant **Z** for a **Zz**-week display.

Zombies

Imagine with the children a land where the people are very different from us. Ask each child to create a zombie from that land. Encourage them to make the zombies weird colors with features different from ours—for example, more or fewer hands, arms, fingers, or toes than we have. Provide a variety of materials for the children to use for these creations. Have the children share them with everyone during circle time.

Zinnias

Show the children a zinnia flower or a picture of one. Provide different colors of paper in four different-size squares for the children to make their own zinnias.

READING AND WRITING READINESS

Zoo Books

Prepare pages for the children to draw zoo animals on. Ask them to take one sheet of paper for each animal they draw. Have them print the animal name on the bottom of the page. When all their drawings are finished, have the children assemble them into a book and add a cover. Help them print, "My Zoo Book by _____" on the cover and decorate it. Staple the books for them. Let the children read their books to each other or invite another class in for them to read to. If the children are ready, ask them to write a simple sentence on each page instead of just a word. An example would be "I see a _____." Provide a word-and-picture chart or dictionaries for the children to use to help them with this project.

Zs from Sticks

Let the children form **Z**s from popsicle sticks or Tinkertoys. Give them a pattern to follow so that they do not reverse the letter while building it. Stress beginning at the left and going to the right.

Zoo Words

Using a chart with words and pictures, have the children write words for things that are found in the zoo. They can either use paper for making words or form them with magnetic or felt letters.

What Has a Zipper?

Gather the children around you to make a list of words for things that zip. Let the children watch as you write these on a large sheet of paper or the chalkboard. Ask them to help you sound out the words. Count how many items you have written with the children and mark that number on the chart.

MATHEMATICS ACTIVITIES

Zebra

Choose a child to be the ringmaster while the other children become zebras and form a circle around the ringmaster. Assign each zebra a different number. The ringmaster calls a zebra by its number. The chosen zebra must stamp a foot the correct number of times. If zebras are right, they gallop around the circle and back to their places. Change the ringmaster and the children's numbers often.

Zebra Stripes

Prepare a game for small groups of children to use. Make pictures of zebras. Give each zebra a different number of stripes. Ask the children to count the stripes and match a number card to each zebra.

SCIENCE ACTIVITIES

Zoo Field Trip

Plan a field trip to the zoo with your class. Prepare by studying different animals you will see, reading books, watching movies and filmstrips about the zoo, and making a list of questions about things the children want to find out. Let the children do projects after the field trip, such as making books or art projects for different animals and matching words and pictures of zoo animals.

Zoo or Not?

Cut out and mount on paper pictures of many different kinds of animals. Have the children sort the pictures according to those that are found in a zoo and those that are not.

Zinnia Seeds

Let the children plant zinnia seeds in little cups that the children decorate with **Z**s. Have them keep the seeds in the sun and water them often to help them grow. Let them keep a chart of drawings indicating the zinnia's growth.

MOVEMENT AND GAMES

Zip the Zebra

Seat the children on the floor in a circle. In the center of the circle, place a big striped ball representing a zebra. Explain that this ball is not to be rolled. Give the children four or five smaller balls that they roll or "zip" into the center of the circle, trying to hit the zebra. If a ball stops in the center, it must remain there until it is knocked back into play by another ball.

Z Movements

Have the children spread out on the play area so they can move without touching anyone else. Ask the children to experiment with these movements as you call them out: zooming, zigzagging, being zebras on all fours, being galloping zebras, and zipping around.

What Am I?

Ask the children to take turns acting out animals that are found in the zoo. As each animal is acted out, write its name on the board.

Zooming

Have the children jump into the air and make a quarter turn to the left. Let them do this four times so they have made a complete turn.

ALPHABET APPETIZER

Zipcorn

Pop a large batch of popcorn. Provide plastic bowls with lids for small groups of children to use. Let them measure into the bowl:

    1 cup popped popcorn
    1 tablespoon warm melted butter
    1 teaspoon wheat germ
    1 tablespoon sunflower seeds
    a few raisins (optional)

Have the children cover the bowl and shake until everything is mixed up. Tell them to put their zipcorn into a cup before eating.

ZIPPY Zs

Cut out this **Z** pattern with the hangers on the top and bottom. Trace around this pattern on other paper to make more **Z**s. Decorate and print **Z**s on both sides of each **Z** hanger. Make them into a chain for **Zz** week.

ZOO ANIMALS

Look at the zoo animal in each box. Print the beginning and ending sound of the animal's name on the lines under the animal. On the back of this paper, draw a little zoo, making 10 of your favorite animals.

___   ___   ___   ___   ___   ___

___   ___   ___   ___   ___   ___

___   ___   ___   ___   ___   ___

Print all the capital letters on the lines. Circle the **Z** with your favorite color.

___ ___ ___ ___ ___ ___ ___ ___ ___ ___

___ ___ ___ ___ ___ ___ ___ ___ ___ ___

___ ___ ___ ___ ___ ___

106